WASHINGTON, D.C.
The Delaplaine
2021 Long Weekend Guide

Andrew Delaplaine

GET 3 *FREE* NOVELS
Like political thrillers?
See next page to download 3 great page-turners—
FREE - no strings attached.

NO BUSINESS HAS PAID A SINGLE PENNY OR GIVEN *ANYTHING* TO BE INCLUDED IN THIS BOOK.

Senior Writer - **James Cubby**

WANT 3 **FREE** THRILLERS?

Why, of course you do!

If you like these writers--
Vince Flynn, Brad Thor, Tom Clancy, James Patterson,
David Baldacci, John Grisham, Brad Meltzer, Daniel Silva,
Don DeLillo

If you like these TV series –
House of Cards, Scandal, West Wing, The Good Wife,

You'll love the **unputdownable** series about
Jack Houston St. Clair, with political intrigue, romance,
and loads of action and suspense.

Madam Secretary, Designated Survivor

Besides writing travel books, I've written political thrillers
for many years that have delighted hundreds of thousands
of readers. I want to introduce you to my work!
Send me an email and I'll send you a link where you can
download the first 3 books in my bestselling series,
absolutely FREE.

Mention **this book** when you email me.

WASHINGTON, D.C.
The Delaplaine
Long Weekend Guide

Chapter 1
WHY WASHINGTON?

DID YOU FIND AN INTERESTING PLACE?
If you discover a place you think I should check out
on my next visit, drop me a line, will you? I'll
mention your name if I end up listing it.
andrewdelaplaine@mac.com

Because it is our nation's Capital where so much
of our history is remembered in national institutions

such as the Smithsonian. If you can't feel like an American here, you're not trying. Walking the Mall or staring up at Lincoln's grim visage sitting in his marble chair. He walked the same path you are walking. It's a very sobering experience to visit the Capital, and something every American should do at least once.

Besides all the marble monuments, imposing edifices and traffic congestion, there's fabulous shopping, lots of free museums, great restaurants, a nightlife scene as active as most other places and vibrantly humming communities living the life of Washington every day and every night.

Politics is to Washington what movies are to L.A., so whatever bar you find yourself in after a long day traipsing through museums, be careful: you might be standing next to a White House assistant or a CIA spy. You never know what will happen in Washington.

Chapter 2
GETTING AROUND

BY CAR

But only if you must. They have gone out of their way to make brining a car downtown one of the worst hassles anywhere in the country. There are speed traps, red light cameras, almost no parking, unannounced street closings, you name it. If you drive here, plan on parking your car and leaving it while you make use of the increasingly user-friend mass transit options. **Personally, I use UBER and LYFT.**

WALKING

No kidding. This is one of the best towns for walking I can think of. Since they've made parking such a hassle downtown, and the public transportation has gotten so good, many people leave their cars at home.

When you use pubic transport to get downtown, you'll find yourself walking a lot anyway because so many of the capital's attractions are strung along the Mall, so the easiest way to get to them is by walking.

The Metro system is good, and with trains, buses and even bikes in common use, getting around is easier than you think.

The Transportation Department has a web site explaining all the options. It's very clear-cut. GoDCgo - www.godcgo.com/

METRO

The Metro is DC's subway system. It's pretty good. It has 5 color-coded lines that are easy to use. Numerous station are downtown where the system runs underground.

METROBUS

A little more complicated for the visitor, but very useful if you can figure out the routes.

Greater Greater Washington

CIRCULATOR BUS

dccirculator.com/

The DC bus system used to be pretty bad, but the circulator Buses are great and very tourist-friendly. They also go places hard to reach by the Metro.

They are like shuttles in the sense that they run on a fairly predictable schedule (every 10 minutes or so) and go between main attractions and the city's most popular neighborhoods for visitors. Costs $1. All D.C. Circulator routes run every ten minutes and cost $1. There are currently five routes.

TAXI
There are hundreds of taxis circulating if you're in a hurry.

Chapter 3
WHERE TO STAY

DID YOU FIND AN INTERESTING PLACE?
If you discover a place you think I should check out
on my next visit, drop me a line, will you? I'll
mention your name if I end up listing it.
andrewdelaplaine@mac.com

DOUBLETREE BY HILTON HOTEL
300 Army Navy Dr., Arlington: 703-416-4100
www.doubletree.hilton.com
This DoubleTree by Hilton Hotel offers a variety of
room types including Deluxe Corner Suites with
balconies. The hotel has five on-site dining options
including the Skydome Lounge, a revolving lounge
perched on the North Tower, and Café Go - a quick
choice for light and healthy meals. Other amenities
include a well-equipped fitness center, an indoor,
heated pool, and free shuttle to the Metro light rail
station. Located near area attractions and local
restaurants.

EMBASSY SUITES
1250 22nd St. NW, Washington DC: 202-857-3388
http://embassysuites3.hilton.com/en/hotels/district-of-
Columbia

Embassy Suites, conveniently located close to historical attractions, Georgetown and downtown business district, offers guests free cooked-to-order breakfast, free Manager's Reception, 24-hour fitness center and indoor pool, whirlpool and game room.

EMBASSY SUITES
1300 Jefferson Davis Hwy., Arlington: 703-979-9799
www.embassysuites.com
Conveniently located near the Pentagon, historic attractions, and a variety of shopping and dining options. Complimentary cooked-to-order breakfast in the tropical atrium. Other amenities include: free Manager's Reception, 24-hour fitness center, indoor pool and spa. One- or two-bedroom suites available with living room, wet bar, and high-speed Internet access. Complimentary airport, Metro, and Crystal City-area shuttle.

FOUR SEASONS HOTEL
2800 Pennsylvania Ave. NW, Washington DC: 202-342-0444
www.fourseasons.com/washington

The Four Seasons Hotel, located among the historical treasures of the nation's capital, is a contemporary standout as the city's only five-star, five-diamond luxury hotel. The hotel offers 222 elegant, modern rooms with an attentive staff. On-site Spa offers guests a variety of relaxing services. You can dine at one of three on-site restaurants: **BOURBON STEAK**, **Season**, and **ENO**. For cocktails visit The Lounge at BOURBON STEAK. Bourbon Steak has a 1000-square-foot garden (that runs along the C&O Canal) that supplies it with dozens of herbs, heirloom tomatoes, chiles and other veggies. You can't go wrong with the chicken-fried veal.

DUPONT CIRCLE HOTEL

1500 New Hampshire Ave. NW, Washington DC: 202-483-6000
www.doylecollection.com
After a $52 million refurbishment, The Dupont Circle Hotel has upped the standard. Within walking distance to the vibrant nightlife of Dupont Circle as well as cafes and bookshops, this luxury hotel offers exceptional accommodations and excellent service. On-site organic influenced restaurant (Café Dupont) and bar (Bar Dupont).

THE HAY-ADAMS
800 16th St. NW, Washington DC: 202-638-6600
www.hayadams.com
The Hay-Adams offers 145 guestrooms, including 21 luxury hotel suites with a variety of room types, different views, amazing beds and pillows with Frette linens, marble baths and English toiletries, classic neutral clean decor, turn-down with slippers & pillow treats. Known as a downtown destination in DC, here you'll find fine dining in a historical setting. The rooftop lounge is a must, great view.

HOTEL PALOMAR
2121 P St. NW, Washington DC: 202-448-1800
www.hotelpalomar-dc.com
Located in Dupont Circle, Kimpton's Hotel Palomar is one of DC's ultimate boutique hotels with 335 guestrooms and suites, most over 500 square feet. Amenities include: on-site restaurant (Urbana

Restaurant & Wine Bar), high-speed wireless Internet access, hosted evening wine reception, fitness center and seasonal outdoor pool. The Palomar is a 100% non-smoking hotel.

HOTEL MONACO
700 F St. NW, Washington DC: 202-628-7177
www.monaco-dc.com
This luxury award-winning AAA Four Diamond boutique hotel is located across from the Smithsonian National Portrait Gallery and steps from attractions like the Verizon Center, the International Spy Museum and National Mall. Amenities include hosted free evening wine reception, morning lobby coffee service, and in-room Spa services. A pet-friendly, 100% non-smoking hotel.

THE JEFFERSON
1200 16th St. NW, Washington, DC: 202-448-2300
www.jeffersondc.com

I could (and have) stayed three days in his hotel and never left it. I was wrapping up one of my political novels set of course in D.C., and had to get it finished. But I had the time to notice every little detail that you can't when you're in a hurry. Like the elegant old plasterwork, the gilding that was in all the right places (what Trump goes for but fails to achieve with his usual sense of design overkill), the elegant lobby, the numerous

antiques, the quiet, respectful, unhurried but yet efficient service. So it's much more than a 99-room luxury boutique hotel that offers modern-day elegance and convenience with 20 elegantly appointed suites, modern amenities, and personalized service. Much more. There's an unforced "quietness" about this place that's completely atypical of most hotels. The hotel features delicious dining at three on-site restaurants (**Plume**, The **Greenhouse** and **Quill**), and sleek spa. Decorated in antiques, period artwork and original documents signed by Thomas Jefferson. Be prepared for a welcoming, professional staff.

KIMPTON CARLYLE DUPONT CIRCLE
1731 New Hampshire Ave NW, Washington, DC, 202-234-3200
www.carlylehoteldc.com
NEIGHBORHOOD: Dupont Circle
Chic newly revamped Art Deco hotel features 198 sleekly appointed guestrooms. Amenities include: Flat-screen TVs, Wi-Fi, and lush Atelier Bloem bath amenities. Hotel features include: Fitness center and on-site eatery at the Riggsby. Located just steps from Dupont Circle. Hosted evening wine bar. Pet-friendly accommodations available.

KIMPTON MASON & ROOK
1430 Rhode Island Ave NW, Washington, DC, 202-742-3100
www.masonandrookhotel.com
NEIGHBORHOOD: Downtown
This hotel offers the feel of fan elegant home, with tweeds and leather funishings. Here guests are pampered with unique services from leopard robes and yoga mats to hosted wine hour and complimentary bikes. On-site fitness center and rooftop pool. The restaurant here is Radiator. Outside there's a big patio and shuffleboard. (When was the last time you played that?) Pet-friendly accommodations.

THE NORMANDY HOTEL

2118 Wyoming Ave. NW, Washington DC: 202-483-1350

www.thenormandydc.com

Located in the heart of DC's embassy belt, this is an ideal location if you're looking see attractions like the White House, the Lincoln Memorial, Capitol Hill and the Smithsonian museums. The hotel offers 75 beautifully appointed guestrooms with LG flat screen & cable TV, mini-fridge, voicemail, work areas, Nespresso coffee facilities, and free high-speed Internet access. Signature rooms are available with access to a garden terrace. Courteous staff.

ROSEWOOD WASHINGTON DC

1050 31st St. NW, Washington DC: 202-617-2400

https://www.rosewoodhotels.com/en/default

Elegant hotel offering polished rooms. Amenities: complimentary Wi-Fi, smart TVs and coffeemakers. 24-hour room service. Onsite features: Spa, gym, upscale restaurant, bar, and rooftop terrace with a bar, lounge, an indoor/outdoor infinity pool. Walking distance from Georgetown Waterfront Park on the Potomac River.

THE SOFITEL
806 15th St NW, Washington, DC, 202-730-8800
www.sofitel.com
NEIGHBORHOOD: Lafayette Square
Luxury hotel offering 237 rooms on 12 floors including 16 suites and one presidential suite.

Amenities include: complimentary Wi-Fi, flat-screen TVs, and minibars. Hotel includes a ballroom, a library (I found a lot of books about Paris and Washington), a fitness center, and onsite restaurant and bar, **Le Bar**, with French-themed cocktails. Conveniently located near well-known restaurants and cafés and Metro Center Metro Station.

W WASHINGTON DC
515 15th St. NW, Washington DC: 202-661-2400
http://www.wwashingtondc.com

This hotel offers a variety of room classes from "wonderful room" to "extremely wow suite." All 317 rooms are designed by Diana Wong and feature the signature W bed, and include amenities like state-of-the-art entertainment, waterfall shower, and a Munchie Box. Other features include the on-site restaurant J&G Steakhouse, P.O.V. rooftop bar and terrace, SWEAT Fitness Center and the capital city's first Bliss Spa. Like any other W, you'll be treated to the Whatever/Whenever service.

THE WATERGATE
2650 Virginia Ave NW Washington DC 202-827-1600
www.thewatergatehotel.com
NEIGHBORHOOD: Foggy Bottom
The totally revamped hotel features 336 luxurious guest rooms and suites. No expense was spared. The hotel staff uniforms were designed by the costume designer for the TV series, "Mad Men." Amenities include: Complimentary Wi-Fi, flat-screen TVs, and custom toiletries. Hotel features on-site dining (casual and fine dining), lobby bar and rooftop bar with views of the Georgetown waterfront, full-service spa, and an indoor pool. Pet-friendly.

Chapter 4
WHERE TO EAT

DID YOU FIND AN INTERESTING PLACE?

If you discover a place you think I should check out on my next visit, drop me a line, will you? I'll mention your name if I end up listing it.
andrewdelaplaine@mac.com

AGORA

1527 17th St. NW, Washington, DC: 202-332-6767
www.agoradc.net
CUISINE: Mediterranean, Greek, Turkish
DRINKS: Full bar
SERVING: Dinner
PRICE RANGE: $$
Another neighborhood spot with a popular happy hour. Besides the typical Mediterranean fare they serve small places like Brussels Sprouts, Zucchini pancakes and Duck Salad, all worth ordering. Good choice for Brunch if you like this type of food. Outdoor patio for warm weather.

THE ARSENAL AT BLUEJACKET

300 Tingey St SE, Washington, DC, 202-524-4862
www.bluejacketdc.com
CUISINE: Traditional American
DRINKS: Full bar
SERVING: Lunch & Dinner – daily; Sunday Brunch;
Closed for lunch on Mon
PRICE RANGE: $$
NEIGHBORHOOD: Navy Yard
Some come to this industrial chic eatery for the great
selection of beers and ales and others come for the
eats and a good time. Menu offers creative American
favorites such as: Pierogi, Wurst Sandwich and
Meatball Stroganoff. Popular date spot. Seating inside
and out – weather permitting.

B TOO

1324 14th St. NW, Washington, DC, 202-627-2800
www.btoo.com
CUISINE: Belgian
DRINKS: Full Bar
SERVING: Lunch, Dinner
PRICE RANGE: $$$
NEIGHBORHOOD: Logan Circle
This beautiful restaurant, showcasing Belgian cuisine
and culture, has two levels with an open kitchen.
Look for owner Bart Vandaele, who competed on
"Top Chef." Great place for brunch as the menu
features nice different types of waffles. Dessert
waffles include a vanilla waffle with ice cream and
chocolate sauce.

for Brunch. Dining room is Beaux Arts design with 30-foot ceilings, period chandeliers and turn of the century elegance. Great service and friendly staff. Top-notch American favorites like Fried Chicken, Pineapple Ham and Catfish Fingers.

BAD SAINT
3226 11th St NW, Washington, No Phone
www.badsaintdc.com
CUISINE: Filipino
DRINKS: Full bar
SERVING: Dinner
PRICE RANGE: $$$
NEIGHBORHOOD: Columbia Heights
Cozy (very intimate—only a couple of dozen seats) upscale Filipino eatery with a rotating menu. Even though the lights seem very bright at night, they are high above you, so the atmosphere is disarmingly intimate. Favorites: Goat braised in lemongrass; Chicken liver mousse; and Purple radishes. Vegetarian options. Creative cocktails. Reservations necessary – booked **months** in advance. (However, I've sometimes lucked into a seat when I walked in, even though I had to wait a bit.)

BAR PILAR

1833 14th St. NW, Washington, DC: 202-265-1751
www.barpilar.com
CUISINE: American, Bar
DRINKS: Full bar
SERVING: Brunch, Lunch, Dinner
PRICE RANGE: $$

Popular two-level bar with Euro-chic ambience. Great brunches but best for late night snacks like tapas and entrees like Roasted Beet Salad and Mussels. Friendly crowd.

BARRACKS ROW

731 8th St SE, Washington, DC, 202-544-3188
www.barracksrow.org

For the past decade, Barracks Row Main Street has worked tirelessly to preserve and enhance Capitol Hill's historic 8th Street, SE, commercial corridor and to revitalize its business community. The group's focus is the five blocks of 8th Street that stretch south from Pennsylvania Ave S.E. to the terminus of 8th Street at the Washington Navy Yard along M Street, S.E. Barracks Row is located eight blocks east of the U.S. Capitol.

BANANA CAFÉ & PIANO BAR

500 8th Street, SE, Washington, DC, 202-543-5906 ·
www.bananacafedc.com
CUISINE: Cuban, Puerto Rican, Tex Mex
DRINKS: Full Bar
SERVING: Lunch, Dinner
PRICE RANGE: $$

NEIGHBORHOOD: Capitol Hill/**Barracks Row**
Tasty food and friendly staff. Great beef burritos.
Outdoor patio and upstairs piano bar.

BEEFSTEAK
800 22nd St. NW, Washington, DC, 202-296-1439
www.beefsteakveggies.com
CUISINE: Fast Food/Vegetarian
DRINKS: No Booze
SERVING: Lunch & Dinner
PRICE RANGE: $$
NEIGHBORHOOD: Foggy Bottom
This healthy eatery from José Andrés' restaurant
group offers a creative menu of veggie & grain bowls.
Salads and vegetables – that's what you'll get here.
When he says beefsteak, he means "beefsteak
tomato." As the chef puts it, "A tomato, an asparagus
or a broccoli is just as powerful as a cow or a
chicken." I couldn't **disagree** with him more.

BELGA CAFÉ
514 8th St. SE, Washington, DC: 202-544-0100
www.belgacafe.com
CUISINE: Belgium
DRINKS: Full bar
SERVING: Lunch, Dinner, Brunch
PRICE RANGE: $$
The original Belgian restaurant in DC. Great
authentic Belgian food and Belgian Beers. Features
an open kitchen, European casual dining room along
with a sidewalk cafe.

BEN'S CHILI BOWL
1213 U St NW Washington, DC, 202-667-0909
www.benschilibowl.com
CUISINE: Hot Dogs, American (Traditional)
DRINKS: No Booze
SERVING: Breakfast, Lunch & Dinner; closed for
Breakfast Sun
PRICE RANGE: $
NEIGHBORHOOD: U Street Corridor
This iconic spot has been around forever and
everyone from Martin Luther King Jr to President
Obama has eaten here. The menu is simple but a great
place to stop for a late night snack. The most popular
item here is the "Half Smoke" – a half beef & half
pork sausage on a bun, topped with mustard, chopped
onions and chili. The second most popular is the
decadent Chili cheese fries. Cash only.

BIRCH & BARLEY
1337 14th St. NW, Washington, DC, 202-567-2576
www.birchandbarley.com
CUISINE: American
DRINKS: Full Bar
SERVING: Breakfast, Lunch, Dinner
PRICE RANGE: $$$
NEIGHBORHOOD: Logan Circle
Comfortable neighborhood type restaurant serving
eclectic fare and an impressive collection of 500
artisan beers (in the upstairs **ChurchKey Bar**).
Delicious menu items like: fried chicken served with
donuts; ruffled herbed mac & cheese; and fig &
prosciutto flatbread.

THE BOMBAY CLUB
815 Connecticut Ave. NW, Washington DC: 202-
659-3727
www.bombayclubdc.com
CUISINE: Indian
DRINKS: Full bar

SERVING: Lunch, Dinner, Brunch
PRICE RANGE: $$$
The Bombay Club emulates characteristics of the old clubs of India serving gourmet Indian cuisine serving four types of Indian cuisine: Parsi Fare, Goan Specialties, Moghlai Specialties, and Coastal Cuisine. Delicious food, good service. Live piano.

BUSBOYS AND POETS
2021 14th St. NW, Washington, DC: 202-387-7638
www.busboysandpoets.com
CUISINE: American
DRINKS: Full bar
SERVING: Breakfast, Brunch
PRICE RANGE: $$
Bookstore and café. A local hangout. Menu includes everything from Fallafel to chicken wings and garlic mashers. Great ambiance and excellent service. Reasonable prices.

BUA THAI CUISINE RESTAURANT & BAR
1635 P St. NW, Washington, DC: 202-265-0828
www.buathai.com
WEBSITE DOWN AT PRESS TIME
CUISINE: Thai
DRINKS: Full bar
SERVING: Lunch, Dinner
PRICE RANGE: $$
Dupont Circle Thai Restaurant with a friendly welcoming atmosphere. Food is almost always good and reasonable. Favorites include: Guong Pad Tang (duck curry) and Gai Ta Kite (grilled pepper

chicken). Good service. Try the upstairs deck if weather permits. Great happy hour specials.

CAFÉ 8
424 8th Street, SE, Washington, DC, 202-547-1555 ·
www.cafe8dc.com
WEBSITE DOWN AT PRESS TIME
CUISINE: Mediterranean
DRINKS: Full Bar
SERVING: Lunch, Dinner
PRICE RANGE: $$
NEIGHBORHOOD: Capitol Hill/Barracks Row
Casual dining with friendly service. Great Turkish food and pizzas. Outdoor dining.

CAFE BERLIN
322 Massachusetts Ave. NE, Washington, DC: 202-543-7656
www.cafeberlin-dc.com

CUISINE: German
DRINKS: Full bar
SERVING: Lunch, Dinner
PRICE RANGE: $$
Located in Capital Hill, this German eatery is a locals' favorite. Typical German fare with dishes like Wiener Schnitzel, gooseberry pie and German beer. Outdoor seating.

CAFÉ MILANO
3251 Prospect St. NW, Washington DC: 202-333-6183
www.cafemilano.net
CUISINE: Italian
DRINKS: Full bar
SERVING: Lunch, Dinner
PRICE RANGE: $$$
This high-end Italian eatery is a favorite of local celebrities, athletes and politicians. If you don't mind "the scene" you'll enjoy the sophisticated atmosphere, great food and excellent service. Wine cellar.

CAFÉ SAINT-EX
1847 14th St. NW, Washington, DC: 202-265-7839
www.saint-ex.com
CUISINE: American
DRINKS: Full bar
SERVING: Lunch, Brunch, Dinner
PRICE RANGE: $$
Here you'll find a cozy pub atmosphere with bar, small dining

area and an outdoor patio. Standard fare with a twist like Roast Chicken, laced with pistachio butter, and Rib-Eye Steak, served with sweet-potato fries. Grilled Tuna also receives raves here. Two levels of seating. Dine early as this place gets packed after 9 p.m.

CAPITOL HILL TANDOOR AND GRILL
419 8th Street, SE, Washington, DC, 202-547-3233
www.capitolhilltandoorandgrill.com
CUISINE: Indian, Pakistani
DRINKS: Full Bar
SERVING: Lunch, Dinner
PRICE RANGE: $$
NEIGHBORHOOD: Capitol Hill/Barracks Row
Delicious Indian cuisine. Menu favorites include: Chicken Tikka Masala and Fish Curry. Indoor and patio dining. Delivery available.

CAVA MEZZE
527 8th Street, SE, Washington, DC, 202-543-9090
www.cavamezze.com
CUISINE: Greek, Mediterranean
DRINKS: Full Bar
SERVING: Lunch, Dinner
PRICE RANGE: $$
NEIGHBORHOOD: Capitol Hill/Barracks Row
Authentic Greek mezze "small plates". Menu favorites include: Crazy feta, Haloumi Sliders, and Saganaki. Indoor and patio dining (in season).

CHIPOTLE MEXICAN GRILL
601 F St. NW, Washington, DC, 202-347-4701
www.chipotle.com

CUISINE: Mexican
DRINKS: No Booze
SERVING: Lunch
PRICE RANGE: $
NEIGHBORHOOD: Georgetown
Mexican fast food fare. Great burritos and tasty tacos.
Always fresh and reportedly the best location of the
chain. Several D.C. locations.

COMMISSARY
1443 P St. NW, Washington, DC: 202-299-0018
www.commissarydc.com
CUISINE: American
DRINKS: Full bar
SERVING: Breakfast, Lunch, Dinner
PRICE RANGE: $$
Located in Logan's Circle. Comfortable and casual
atmosphere. Sofas, lots of TVs and free WiFi. Great
breakfast and popular happy hour. Menu features
everything from authentic tacos (hard to find in DC),
breakfast quesadillas, chicken nachos and vegetarian
options.

Trelissed garden at The Dabney

DABNEY
122 Blagden Aly NW, Washington, 202-450-1015
www.thedabney.com
CUISINE: American (New)
DRINKS: Full bar
SERVING: Dinner
PRICE RANGE: $$$
NEIGHBORHOOD: Shaw, Downtown
Set in a former row house, this rustic eatery offers a
menu of Mid-Atlantic cuisine, sourced from the very
finest purveyors, farmers and fishermen in the area.
They get great use out of the wood-burning hearth—
some of the food is cooked just the way they did it

200 years ago. You can see everything going on in the open kitchen. Menu picks: Sorghum-glazed short rib and Catfish sliders. Many of the dishes are meant to share. Has a few seats outdoors.

DEL MAR
791 Wharf St SW, Washington, 202-525-1402
www.delmardc.com
CUISINE: Spanish / Seafood
DRINKS: Full bar
SERVING: Lunch, Dinner
PRICE RANGE: $$$
NEIGHBORHOOD: Southwest DC

Spanish villa-like eatery offers an upscale dining experience. The chef's other restaurants are Italian, but this one focuses on Spanish coastal cuisine, so lots of flavorful seafood dishes. (His business partner was born in Spain.) Chef is a James Beard winner & also Michelin-starred. As stuffy as all that sounds, the mood here is just the opposite—lively, fun, busy. Favorites: Calamari paella and Basque tapas. Nice wine selection – amazing sangria. Waterfront views.

DISTRICT COMMONS
2200 Pennsylvania Ave. NW, Washington DC: 202-587-8277
www.districtcommonsdc.com
CUISINE: American
DRINKS: Full bar
SERVING: Lunch, Dinner, Brunch
PRICE RANGE: $$

This is a 21st Century take on the traditional American tavern. Anchored by a monumental raw bar and an open-hearth oven for flatbreads and savory tarts. Classics served include ham and biscuits, chili glazed duck, brick pressed chicken, and classic hanger steak.

DUPONT ITALIAN KITCHEN
1637 17th St. NW, Washington, DC: 202-328-3222
www.dupontitaliankitchen.com
CUISINE: Italian, Pizza
DRINKS: Full bar
SERVING: Lunch, Dinner, Brunch
PRICE RANGE: $$
This place has a big gay following but a locals' favorite. Indoor and outdoor seating. Food is good and service is excellent (most of the time). Big portions. Great pizza and tiramisu to die for.

EL SAPO CUBAN SOCIAL CLUB

8455 Fenton St, Silver Spring, MD, 301-326-1063
www.elsaporestaurant.com
CUISINE: Cuban
DRINKS: Full Bar
SERVING: Dinner
PRICE RANGE: $$

Out of the Beltway over in Silver Spring is this
modern eatery serving classic Cuban fare. Being from
Miami, I know the real thing when I see it. Or eat it,
that is. This place is bright, colorful, fun and busy.
Favorites: Ropa Vieja (a beef dish that means 'old
clothes,' don't ask me why) and Berro, Field Greens
& No Oil salad. Happy hour specials. Nice homestyle
Cuban desserts.

EL TAMARINDO

1785 Florida Ave NW, Washington, DC, 202-328-3660

www.eltamarindodc.com

CUISINE: Salvadoran / Mexican

DRINKS: Full Bar

SERVING: Lunch, Dinner

PRICE RANGE: $$

Popular late-night eatery (though it's open all day) with a creative menu of Salvadoran and Mexican cuisine. I recommend ordering the Salvadoran dishes over the Mexican—you can get Mexican food anywhere in the country, but not Salvadoran cuisine. This place has been around since the early 1980s. They've thrown everything from somebody's attic onto each inch of wall space in the little restaurant, and even from the ceiling you'll find flags handing down, posters everywhere, little pieces of bric-a-brac. Very busy on the eye. But colorful, very colorful. I'd say nothing they've put on the wall since they opened has even been taken down. My Favorites: Beef empanadas and Revuelta (pork & cheese) pupusas. If you didn't know already, a pupusa is a robust cake or flatbread cooked on a griddle and made from cornmeal or rice, usually cornmeal. Into this humble piece of bread they stuff various ingredients, basically whatever you have in the house. But in a restaurant you have choices, from cheese to pork rinds to refried beans to squash or whatever. Authentic places serve cole slaw with a pupusa, but it's a spicier cole slaw than we see in the U.S. In El Salvador, they eat pupusas with their hands, not forks, and you can too. This place offers complimentary chips and salsa.

ESTADIO
1520 14th St. NW, Washington, DC, 202-319-1404
www.estadio-dc.com
CUISINE: Spanish, Tapas
DRINKS: Full Bar
SERVING: Lunch, Dinner
PRICE RANGE: $$$
NEIGHBORHOOD: Logan Circle
Friendly restaurant with an open kitchen so you can see the food being prepared. Great tapas. Chef Haidar Karoumi's menu favorites include: roasted sweet-corn salad and a bocadilllo—a small sandwich on home-baked bread with crispy pork belly and pickled shishito pepper. Impressive wine list with more than 400 wines, most from Spain.

FIREFLY

1310 New Hampshire Ave. NW, Washington, DC:
202-861-1310
www.firefly-dc.com
CUISINE: American, Organic, Gluten-free
DRINKS: Full bar
SERVING: Brunch, Lunch, Dinner
PRICE RANGE: $$
Neighborhood restaurant in downtown DC near
Dupont Circle featuring local, organic menu and
American comfort food. Great a la carte brunch from
a gluten free menu that included cheesy grits, bacon
and fruit cup. Great service. Sandwiches, salads,
entrees.

FLORIDA AVENUE GRILL

1100 Florida Ave NW, Washington, DC, 202-265-1586
www.floridaavenuegrill.com
CUISINE: Diner/Soul Food
DRINKS: No Booze
SERVING: Breakfast, Lunch & Dinner
PRICE RANGE: $$
NEIGHBORHOOD: U Street Corridor
Open since 1944, local greasy spoon serves up simple menu of diner fare and down-home Southern classics. This place has lots of character and so does the food. Dishes like Fried catfish over grits with 2 sunny side up eggs – delicious. Other Southern favorites like Pan fried chicken and Smothered pork chops.

FOUNDING FARMERS
1924 Pennsylvania Ave NW, Washington, DC, 202-822-8783
www.wearefoundingfarmers.com
CUISINE: American Traditional
DRINKS: Full bar
SERVING: Breakfast, Lunch & Dinner
PRICE RANGE: $$
NEIGHBORHOOD: Foggy Bottom
Co-op owned American eatery with a menu of creative comfort food that's enjoyed with the same gusto by suited lobbyists as well as blue collar workers. Menu favorites include: Spicy Ahi Tuna Poke and Glazed Cedar Plank Salmon. Great place for breakfast—the beignets are made to order. Try the red velvet pancakes with cinnamon syrup and whipped cream cheese butter. Your arteries will not thank you, but your stomach will.

FOX & HOUNDS LOUNGE

1537 17th St. NW, Washington, DC: 202-232-6307
www.triofoxandhounds.com
CUISINE: American
DRINKS: Full bar
SERVING: Dinner, Breakfast, Brunch
PRICE RANGE: $
A good hangout with reasonable prices. Outdoor
seating, perfect for people watching on a warm night.
Good selection of nosh food like the Crab Cake
Sandwich, Portobello Sandwich and Chicken
Tenders. Also entrees like Lobster Dinner. Drinkers
rejoice at the heavy pours.

GEORGIA BROWN'S

950 15th St. NW, Washington, DC: 202-393-4499

www.gbrowns.com
CUISINE: Southern
DRINKS: Full bar
SERVING: Brunch, Lunch, Dinner

PRICE RANGE: $$$
If you're a fan of Southern cuisine then this is the place. You'll find dishes like: Fried Green Tomatoes, Charleston Perlau, Louisiana Devil Shrimp and Southern Fried Chicken. Don't forget to order a Mint Julep. Live jazz on Wednesday nights. Great service.

GHIBELLINA
1610 14th St. NW, Washington, DC, 202-803-2389
www.ghibellina.com
CUISINE: Italian
DRINKS: Full Bar
SERVING: Dinner

PRICE RANGE: $$$
NEIGHBORHOOD: Logan Circle
A fairly new Italian Gastro Pub that calls itself a traditional Tuscan trattoria. A friendly atmosphere and a menu that includes favorites like: Carpaccio de Piovra, eggplant, and kale pesto gnocchi. The homemade gelato should not be passed up. Great wine list and good service.

GOOD STUFF EATERY
303 Pennsylvania Ave. SE, Washington DC: 202-543-8222
www.goodstuffeatery.com
CUISINE: Burgers
DRINKS: Beer & Wine
SERVING: Lunch, Dinner
PRICE RANGE: $$
Good delicious American food like handcrafted burgers, hand-cut fries, handspun shakes and farm fresh salads made with the highest quality ingredients.

HANK'S OYSTER BAR
1624 Q St NW, Washington, DC, 202-462-4265
633 Pennsylvania Ave SE, Washington, DC, 202-733-1971
www.hanksoysterbar.com
CUISINE: Seafood
DRINKS: Full bar
SERVING: Lunch & Dinner
PRICE RANGE: $$
NEIGHBORHOOD: Dupont Circle
Like a spot you'd find in New England, this bar offers up a great selection of seafood, clams, lobster rolls,

raw bar, Chesapeake Bay rockfish (which happens to be Maryland's official state fish—who knew?) with a rotating list of daily specials. They even have their own oyster specially cultivated for this restaurant—the **Hayden's Reef**, an oyster they worked to develop with Dragon Creek Aqua Farm. Make sure you try a side order of the Old Bay Fries, lightly covered with the unique Maryland spice mix. Great happy hour deals. Main dining room, outdoor seating and three bar areas.

JALEO
480 7th St NW Washington, DC, 202-628-7949
www.jaleo.com/dc
CUISINE: Spanish, Tapas
DRINKS: Full Bar
SERVING: Lunch, Dinner
PRICE RANGE: $$$
NEIGHBORHOOD: Penn Quarter

This ever-popular eatery is the flagship enterprise of the world-famous Chef Jose Andres. Yes, folks, it all grew from this joint. Well, it's not quite a 'joint.' It's sleek, modern, stylish, and not as pricey as you might expect for a Jose Andres eatery. Here they serve his traditional Spanish fare like tapas, paella and sangria. Everything, of course, is expertly prepared because Jose Andres is nothing if not picky. Favorites: Salpicón de cangrejo (jumbo lump crab, cucumbers, peppers, tomatoes, cauliflower & a hefty dose of brandy sauce) and Tortilla de patatas al momento (Spanish omelette, potatoes, onions). Delicious Spanish desserts. I'd recommend reserving ahead.

JAVA HOUSE DC
1645 Q St., NW, Washington, DC: 202-387-6622
www.javahousedc.net
CUISINE: Coffee, Tea
DRINKS: No Alcohol
SERVING: Coffee, snacks.
PRICE RANGE: $$$
It's all about the location here, the best thing about Java House. Excellent coffee – beans roasted on premises, fresh bagels, poor service.

JOHNNY'S HALF-SHELL
1819 Columbia Rd NW, Washington, 202-506-5257
www.johnnyshalfshell.net
CUISINE: Seafood
DRINKS: Full bar
SERVING: Dinner
PRICE RANGE: $$
NEIGHBORHOOD: Adams Morgan
With a name like Johnny's Half-Shell, you'd think this was a fish shack like you see scattered along Cape Code. Wrong. This popular (and very fun) neighborhood eatery specializing in seafood specialties boasts a James Beard award-winning chef, and rightly so. Super delicious seafood. Favorites: Lobster Roll sliders and Grilled Cobia Fillet. Happy Hours specials. Indoor & patio seating.

KITH AND KIN
801 Wharf St SW, Washington, 202-878-8566
www.kithandkindc.com
CUISINE: African / Caribbean / American (New)
DRINKS: Full bar
SERVING: Breakfast, Lunch, Dinner
PRICE RANGE: $$$
NEIGHBORHOOD: District Wharf
Located inside the **InterContinental**, Chef
Onwuachi's (another of DC's James Beard winners)
upscale Afro-Caribbean eatery offers a unique menu
featuring goat, oxtail & seafood dishes. Since DC is a
majority black city, it only makes sense to celebrate
some African heritage. Nothing could be more
splendid that the chef's food in this sleek modern
restaurant. He takes traditional dishes (think jerk
chicken) and dresses them up, expanding their reach

with his innovative talent. (He worked at Per Se and Eleven Madison Park in New York, so he knows his stuff.) Favorites: Braised oxtails and Moroccan Spiced Pork Belly. Great cocktails. Main dining room and lounge.

KRAMERBOOKS & AFTERWORDS CAFÉ
1517 Connecticut Ave. NW, Washington, DC: 202-387-1400
www.kramers.com
CUISINE: Café fare
DRINKS: Full bar
SERVING: Breakfast, Sunday Brunch, lunch, desserts
PRICE RANGE: $$
Bookstore with café open since 1976. First Bookstore/Café in the country to feature cappuccino, espresso, a full bar and food. An institution with locals. Live music Wed. – Sat.

LA TOMATE
1701 Connecticut Ave. NW, Washington DC: 202-667-5505
www.latomatebistro.com
CUISINE: Italian
DRINKS: Full bar
SERVING: Lunch, Dinner, Brunch
PRICE RANGE: $$
A friendly neighborhood bistro that serves affordable regional Italian cuisine. Great views on the patio. New Prosciutto Bar. Quality service and excellent food.

LAOS IN TOWN

250 K St NE, Washington, DC, 202-864-6620
www.laosintown.com
CUISINE: Laotian / Vegan
DRINKS: Full Bar
SERVING: Lunch, Dinner
PRICE RANGE: $$
This is a popular eatery offering classic Laotian cuisine. There's a separate menu for hard-core vegans. The interior here is modern, clean, sharp-edged. There's plenty of outdoor seating and I'd sit out there if the weather permits. Favorites: Grilled beef and Khua mee (which is a dish of sweet fried noodles). Interesting desserts like Khao Niao (that's a hot mango pudding).

LAURIOL PLAZA

1835 18th St. NW, Washington, DC: 202-387-0035
www.lauriolplaza.com

CUISINE: Latin American, Spanish, Tex-Mex
DRINKS: Full bar
SERVING: Lunch, Dinner
PRICE RANGE: $$
Great Mexican fare and delicious margaritas (Voted Best Margaritas by Washington City Magazine – 2011). Try the Pechuga De Pollo, the Derango Platter and the sangriarita – the perfect combination of a margarita and sangria. Huge restaurant with dining room and upstairs patio. Excellent service.

LAVAGNA
539 8th St SE, Washington, DC, 202-546-5006
www.lavagnadc.com
CUISINE: Italian
DRINKS: Full Bar

SERVING: Lunch, Dinner
PRICE RANGE: $$
NEIGHBORHOOD: Capitol Hill/Barracks Row
Fresh Italian fare in a friendly atmosphere. Popular spot for Sunday brunch with lots of specials and menu favorites like Goat and Pepper Preserve Omelet with unlimited mimosas.

LE DIPLOMATE
1601 14th St NW Washington, DC, 202-332-3333
www.lediplomatedc.com
CUISINE: French café
DRINKS: Full Bar
SERVING: Breakfast, Lunch, Dinner, Brunch
PRICE RANGE: $$$
NEIGHBORHOOD: Logan Circle
A celebration of the French café serving everything from the classic Onion Soup Gratinee to Steak Frites

and Escargots. Delicious desserts. Tasty crusty baguettes made in-house. Reservations recommended.

LITTLE SEROW
1511 17th St NW, Washington, DC, 202-332-9200
www.littleserow.com
CUISINE: Thai
DRINKS: Beer & Wine Only
SERVING: Dinner
PRICE RANGE: $$$
NEIGHBORHOOD: Dupont Circle
A great Thai-inspired restaurant run by Chef Johnny Monis that consistently gets rave reviews. (His other restaurant, **KOMI**, is Greek, like Johnny.) The chef will send out to your table 6 or 7 dishes to be served family-style. Menu favorites include Khao tang gapi (salted prawn/cilantro/peanut with fried rice cake) and Ma hor (sour fruit and dried shrimp served with palm sugar).

LOCAL 16
1602 U St. NW, Washington, DC: 202-265-2828
www.localsixteen.com
CUISINE: American
DRINKS: Full bar
SERVING: Lunch, Dinner
PRICE RANGE: $$
Popular neighborhood restaurant that serves farm-driven, classic American fare. Here you'll find Pan Roasted Chicken and Wood-Fire Artisan Pizzas. Second floor lounge with heated rooftop patio. Basically it's comfort food and nothing special.

Check out the Facebook Fan Brunch on Sundays (make reservations).

LOGAN TAVERN
1423 P St. NW, Washington, DC: 202-332-3710
www.logantavern.com
CUISINE: Bar, Burgers, American
DRINKS: Full bar
SERVING: Lunch, Dinner, Brunch
PRICE RANGE: $$
Local tavern with friendly crowd. Great place for brunch. Good food, good service. Popular spot for dinner. Dinner menu

selections include: Ginger Calamari - Flash Fried, Buffalo Shrimp with Spicy Blue Cheese Sauce, Portabella & Eggplant Sandwich with Feta Cheese and Sun-Dried Tomato Pesto, and 'Big Texas' Grilled Burger & Slow Roasted BBQ Brisket with Cheddar & Red Onions.

LOLA'S BARRACKS BAR AND GRILL

711 8th St SE, Washington, DC, 202-547-5652
www.lolasthehill.com
WEBSITE DOWN AT PRESS TIME
CUISINE: American
DRINKS: Full Bar
SERVING: Lunch, Dinner, Late Night
PRICE RANGE: $$
NEIGHBORHOOD: Capitol Hill/Barracks Row
This comfortable grill with a pub-like atmosphere offers a great place for a quick lunch or dinner. Menu favorites include: Chicken salad sandwich, sliders, and fish tacos. Friendly service.

DID YOU FIND AN INTERESTING PLACE?

If you discover a place you think I should check out on my next visit, drop me a line, will you? I'll mention your name if I end up listing it.
andrewdelaplaine@mac.com

MAKETTO
1351 H St NE, Washington, 202-838-9972
www.maketto1351.com
CUISINE: Cambodian / Taiwanese
DRINKS: Full bar
SERVING: Breakfast, Lunch, Dinner
PRICE RANGE: $$
NEIGHBORHOOD: H Street Corridor
Popular modern creative spot that combines 3 things
and does it very well in my opinion: a marketplace
featuring a restaurant and coffee shop as well as a
fashion boutique selling designer duds. The restaurant
has a chef that throws together the wild tastes of both

Cambodia and Taiwan. The flavors jump out at you when you first come in the place as the aromas of a dozen different spices fill the air. Favorites: Braised pork steamed bao; Grilled marinated duck hearts (I know, it sounds awful, but it's damned good); and Num Pang Sandwich with pork shoulder. Nice outdoor seating area where you can get away from the busy things going on inside the shop.

MARTIN'S TAVERN
1264 Wisconsin Ave. NW, Washington, DC, 202-333-7370;
www.martinstavern.com
CUISINE: American
DRINKS: Full Bar
SERVING: Lunch, Dinner
PRICE RANGE: $$
NEIGHBORHOOD: Georgetown
A historic family-owned tavern with mismatched Tiffany-style lamps hanging over the mahogany bar. American menu serves items like Richard M. Nixon's favorite meatloaf and President Truman's preferred pot roast.

MATCHBOX
521 8th Street, SE, Washington, DC, 202-548-0369
www.matchboxrestaurants.com
CUISINE: Pizza, American
DRINKS: Full Bar
SERVING: Lunch, Dinner
PRICE RANGE: $$
NEIGHBORHOOD: Capitol Hill/Barracks Row
Sliders, pizza, American food

Friendly neighborhood spot with great food and great service. Good wine and beer menu. Menu favorites include: Fire & Smoke pizza and the sliders. Patio seating that's dog-friendly.

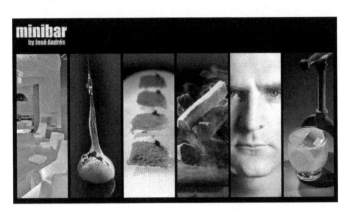

MINIBAR
855 E St. NW, Washington DC: 202-393-0812
www.minibarbyjoseandres.com
CUISINE: American
DRINKS: Full bar
SERVING: Dinner
PRICE RANGE: $$$$
Ranked #1 by Washington City Paper's list of most powerful restaurants. An imaginative menu in an intimate setting. Don't miss out on this dining experience.

NOOSHI
524 8th St SE, Washington, DC, 202-827-8832
www.nooshidc.com
CUISINE: American, Sushi
DRINKS: Full Bar

SERVING: Lunch, Dinner
PRICE RANGE: $$
NEIGHBORHOOD: Capitol Hill/Barracks Row
Newly opened eatery with impressive Asian Fusion
menu. Great food and friendly service. Menu
favorites include: noodle Bowl with the Pork Loin,
Drunken noodles, and general tao chicken.

OBELISK
2029 P St NW, Washington DC: 202-872-1180
www.obeliskdc.com
CUISINE: Italian
DRINKS: Full bar
SERVING: Dinner
PRICE RANGE: $$$$
One of the best dining experiences in DC. Delicious
food and friendly service. Obelisk is a dining
pleasure! Unique and inventive menu. Impressive
wine selections.

OLD EBBITT GRILL
675 15th St NW, Washington, DC, 202-347-4800

www.ebbitt.com
CUISINE: American
DRINKS: Full Bar
SERVING: Breakfast, Lunch, Dinner
PRICE RANGE: $$
NEIGHBORHOOD: McPherson Square
This beautiful restaurant is a historic DC landmark. Good food and excellent service. I seldom come to DC without grabbing a seat at the bar and slurping down 2 or 3 dozen ice cold oysters. Menu favorites include: Crispy shrimp tacos, Seared Atlantic Salmon and Trout Parmesan.

OYAMEL COCINA MEXICANA
401 7th St NW, Washington, DC, 202-628-1005
www.oyamel.com
CUISINE: Mexican/Tapas Bar
DRINKS: Full bar
SERVING: Lunch & Dinner
PRICE RANGE: $$$
NEIGHBORHOOD: Penn Quarter
Upscale Mexican (not Tex-Mex) eatery offering a menu of creative Mexican fare and street food, but always with a more sophisticated approach than a street vendor would bring to the task. Tacos have Yucatan-style BBQ pork, Mexican sour orange and pickled red onion, for instance. Or try the mushroom sautéed with cream sauce and served with potato chips. Nice selection of cocktails and wine. Food served in small plates – ceviches and tacos.

PEARL DIVE OYSTER PALACE
1612 14th St. N.W., Washington, DC, 202-319-1612

www.pearldivedc.com
CUISINE: Seafood
DRINKS: Full Bar
SERVING: Dinner, Brunch
PRICE RANGE: $$$

NEIGHBORHOOD: Logan Circle
This very popular local hangout with its beat-up furniture, a floor that could use a little varnish and the big window overlooking the street, serves great seafood and some of the freshest oysters in town. (If I'm not at the Old Ebbitt Grill swallowing oysters, I can be found here.) If you're not into raw oysters then try the wood-grilled oysters with garlic, red chili butter and gremolata. Or my go-to dish: the cornmeal crusted ousters with Andouille sausage, served with a sweet potato hash. Late night menu. Bar on the second floor.

THE PIG
1320 14th St. NW (bet. N. Rhode Island Ave & N. N St), 202-290-2821
www.thepigdc.com/
CUISINE: New American; pork focus
DRINKS: full bar, happy hour 3-7
SERVING: lunch weekdays till 4; weekend brunch; dinner nightly.
PRICE RANGE: $$$
They have their own farm in Maryland that the vegetables served here come from. Menu is focused on pork and all the great things you can do with it. Radish & arugula salad, charred caesar (with duck egg and grilled cheese-anchovy croutons), roasted beets. Pig dish favorites: braised cheek, wild boar ragu over pappardelle, pulled pork mac n cheese, pork & lamb meatballs served over grits in a stewed tomato sauce.

PIZZA PARADISO
2003 P St. NW, Washington DC: 202-223-1245
3282 M St. NW, Washington DC: 202-337-1245
www.eatyourpizza.com
CUISINE: Pizza
DRINKS: Full bar
SERVING: Lunch, Dinner
PRICE RANGE: $$
Great pizza, friendly bartenders, and fun atmosphere. Beware of the lines and the noise level but overall very comfortable. Impressive beer selection.

POCA MADRE
777 I St NW, Washington, 202-838-5300
www.pocamadredc.com
CUISINE: Mexican
DRINKS: Full bar
SERVING: Dinner

PRICE RANGE: $$$
NEIGHBORHOOD: Chinatown
Trendy eatery offering upscale Mexican cuisine in a
great atmosphere—soft-hued wooden floors,
interesting wall treatments, plants hanging from the
walls in little planters. The chef comes from a Cuban
dad and a Peruvian mom, so he brings these disparate
influences as he focuses on Mexican cuisine. Menu
picks: Hamachi Tostada and Pato al Pastor (slow
roasted whole duck—it's worth getting—take what
you can't eat home, that's what I did). Creative
cocktails. Outdoor lounge area.

THE PRIME RIB

2020 K St. NW, Washington DC: 202-466-8811
www.theprimerib.com
CUISINE: Steakhouse, Seafood
DRINKS: Full bar
SERVING: Lunch, Dinner
PRICE RANGE: $$$$
Zagat's #1 Rated Steakhouse in DC. The Prime Rib
features USDA Prime Dry Aged NY Strip Steaks &
USDA Filet Mignon. Casual dress at lunch, jackets
after 5 p.m. Live piano music nightly.

QUEEN'S ENGLISH
3410 11th St NW, Washington, No Phone
www.queensenglishdc.com
CUISINE: Hong Kong-style cafe
DRINKS: Full bar
SERVING: Dinner; Closed Sun & Mon
PRICE RANGE: $$$
NEIGHBORHOOD: Columbia Heights
Upscale but at the same time charming and intimate spot offering Hong Kong cuisine on a unique and ever-changing menu. Take a good look at the colorful wallpaper with bursting colors that remind me motifs in Chinese art I've seen over the years. Favorites: Soy braised enoki mushroom; Twice cooked pork rib. Impressive wine list.

RAPPAHANNOCK OYSTER BAR
1309 5th St. NE, Washington, DC, 202-544-4702
www.rroysters.com
CUISINE: Seafood, Bar
DRINKS: Beer and Wine only

SERVING: Lunch, Dinner
PRICE RANGE: $$
Inside the busy-as-ever Union Market is this small bar
with countertop that seats about 12. Small menu with
items like great fresh oysters, crab cakes and beer.
This place is run by one of the oldest family-operated
Chesapeake Bay oyster families, so the product they
bring in—the Olde Salts oysters and the soft
Rappahannocks variety—are all great.

RASIKA
633 D St. NW, Washington, DC: 202-637-1222
1190 New Hampshire Ave. NW, Washington DC:
202-466-2500
www.rasikarestaurant.com
CUISINE: Indian
DRINKS: Full bar
SERVING: Lunch, Dinner
PRICE RANGE: $$$
Excellent Indian restaurant with a fine dining
experience. Vegan selections. Delicious entrees like

the Papeta Ringna Nu Shak, which is potatoes and Indian eggplant cooked with mustard seeds in a tomato sauce and topped with cilantro. If you're a fan of Indian food then this is the place. Make reservations.

RISTORANTE TOSCA

1112 F St NW, Washington, DC, 202-367-1990
www.toscadc.com
CUISINE: Italian
DRINKS: Full bar
SERVING: Lunch & Dinner; Dinner only on Sat; closed Sun – dress nicely.
PRICE RANGE: $$$
NEIGHBORHOOD: Downtown
Upscale dining featuring waiters in formal uniforms serving from a menu of fine Northern Italian fare. Definitely a place for serious grownups, no kids. Half the bills that actually get through Congress are probably discussed here first, by lobbyists paying for every meal. You're first impressed by the "beigeness" of the room—muted colors of saddle, khaki, camel, ecru, biscuit, tan, cream—you get the idea. Nothing too jolting. Don't raise your voice. By all means choose the pasta here—it's sublime. Menu favorites include: Lobster ravioli and Bucatini. Very attentive service. Crunchy bread, good coffee from a French press. Great wine list.

ROOSTER & OWL
2436 14th St NW, Washington, 202-813-3976
www.roosterowl.com
CUISINE: American (New)
DRINKS: Full bar
SERVING: Dinner; Closed Sun & Mon
PRICE RANGE: $$$
NEIGHBORHOOD: Columbia Heights
Popular eatery featuring market-driven New
American cuisine. Big emphasis on fresh vegetables,
and they prepare everything expertly. Has an
affordable pre-fixe menu that I usually select when
I'm here. Sharing plates also popular. Fun place with
a good vibe. You get that, "I'm glad I chose this
place" feeling when you sit down. Favorites: Short
Rib and Maryland crab cake. Wine pairings available.

ROSE'S LUXURY
717 8th St SE, Washington, DC, 202-580-8889
www.rosesluxury.com
CUISINE: American (New)/Pastas

DRINKS: Full bar
SERVING: Dinner; closed Sun
PRICE RANGE: $$$
NEIGHBORHOOD: Capital Hill
Located in a converted townhouse, this eatery features a creative menu of New American tapas and an upstairs lounge. If you don't want to wait for a table, you can eat at the kitchen counter facing the open kitchen. Menu changes often but some of the popular dishes include: Pork & lychee salad and Grilled Veal. Arrive early as this place gets packed. Reservations recommended.

RUSSIA HOUSE
1800 Connecticut Ave NW, Washington, DC, 202-234-9433

www.russiahouselounge.com
CUISINE: Russian
DRINKS: Full Bar
SERVING: Dinner
PRICE RANGE: $$$
NEIGHBORHOOD: Dupont Circle
This restaurant/lounge lives up to its name with its extensive list of vodkas. Try the sampler which lets you select any 5 vodkas to taste. Nice menu. Favorites include: Potato Mushroom Cocotte, Chicken Kiev, and Vareniki and Cauliflower. Excellent service.

DID YOU FIND AN INTERESTING PLACE?
If you discover a place you think I should check out on my next visit, drop me a line, will you? I'll mention your name if I end up listing it.
andrewdelaplaine@mac.com

SEVEN REASONS
2208 14th St NW, Washington, 202-290-2630
www.sevenreasonsdc.com
CUISINE: Latin American
DRINKS: Full bar
SERVING: Dinner; Closed on Mondays
PRICE RANGE: $$$

NEIGHBORHOOD: NorthWest

Old brick walls give a warm feeling in this multi-level eatery that offers a unique culinary experience with a great interior décor. These Latin-inspired dishes are meant to be shared. Prepared by a Venezuelan chef, he brings all the influences of Venezuela (Spanish, Italian, Indian, Chinese) that are reflected in the highly diverse cuisine of that country. The chef (like most Uber drivers I have in Miami) fled Venezuela's political & social turmoil for a better place—and he ended up here in DC where he's got this truly fabulous restaurant. Visit him. You'll love it as much as I did. Favorites: Lamb loin palo-a-pique; Swordfish belly and trout roe; and Royal sea bass ceviche.

THE SOURCE

575 Pennsylvania Ave. NW, Washington DC: 202-637-6100

www.wolfgangpuck.com/restaurants/fine-dining

CUISINE: Asian Fusion, American

DRINKS: Full bar

SERVING: Lunch, Dinner

PRICE RANGE: $$$$

Wolfgang Puck puts his mark on this fine dining DC restaurant. A three-level restaurant that offers two dining experiences, one casual, the other fine dining. Good service.

SPOKEN ENGLISH
1770 Euclid St NW, Washington, DC, 202-588-0525
www.spokenenglishdc.com
CUISINE: Asian Fusion
DRINKS: Full Bar
SERVING: Dinner; Closed Sunday & Monday
PRICE RANGE: $$$

Spoken English is a Japanese inspired eatery offering a unique dining experience because it's one of those 'stand-at-the-bar-and-eat' places the Japanese call *tachinomiya*. The restaurant part of the place is inseparable from the kitchen, and actually *is* a part of the kitchen, and there are only two tables where you can stand. Even though the place is quite tiny, it's doesn't feel claustrophobic in the least. Plus, if you want to be elbow-to-elbow with somebody, this is definitely the place to go. Menu offers sake selections and Asian street style dishes. Just point to most anything on the menu and you'll probably like it. I did. But my Favorites are the Chicken skin dumpling and Chicken Yakitori. Creative cocktails. Reservations recommended.

SWEETGREEN
1512 Connecticut Ave. NW, Washington DC, 202-387-9338
www.sweetgreen.com
CUISINE: Ice Cream & Frozen Yogurt, Fruits & Veggies
DRINKS: No Booze
SERVING: Lunch
PRICE RANGE: $$
NEIGHBORHOOD: Dupont Circle
Salad bar with a unique selection of locally sourced vegetables mixed into combinations like spicy sabzi, a mixture of baby spinach, roasted broccoli, quinoa, a squirt of sriracha and chile-carrot vinaigrette. Interesting selection of healthy beverages.

TED'S BULLETIN
505 8th St SE, Washington, DC, 202-544-8337
www.tedsbulletin.com
CUISINE: American
DRINKS: Full Bar
SERVING: Breakfast, Lunch, Dinner
PRICE RANGE: $$
NEIGHBORHOOD: Capitol Hill/Barracks Row
A popular spot with a retro-diner feel serving
American favorites like tomato soup and grilled
cheese sandwiches. Speaking of retro, the homemade
twinkies and pop-tarts. Great milkshakes. They also
have "cocktail" milkshakes, like the Dirty Girl Scout,
tarted up with peppermint schnapps.

THIP KHAO
3462 14th St NW, Washington, 202-387-5426
www.thipkhao.com
CUISINE: Laotian
DRINKS: Full bar
SERVING: Lunch, Dinner
PRICE RANGE: $$
NEIGHBORHOOD: Columbia Heights
Modern eatery offering genuine Laotian cuisine.
Nothing particularly intriguing about the interior here.
What brought me here was the food, because it's very
difficult to get genuine Laotian cuisine prepared by
somebody who knows what they're doing. What
you'll find here is the real thing. Special fish and pork
dishes, some of which have red hot spices that will
burn your tongue off. (Stay away from the Red Goat
Curry! I'm sure I'd have like it if I could've tasted it,
LOL.) Super inventive salad bursting with fresh and
different flavor combinations. Favorites: Khao siin;

Crispy coconut-rice salad with fermented pork (nam khao). Classic cocktails.

TOKI UNDERGROUND
1234 H St NE, Washington, DC, 202-388-3086
www.tokiunderground.com
CUISINE: Asian Fusion
DRINKS: Full Bar
SERVING: Dinner
PRICE RANGE: $$
NEIGHBORHOOD: H Street Corridor/Atlas District/Near Northeast
A trendy Taiwanese-style ramen bar decorated with skateboards and featuring punk/indie music. Authentic ramen dishes such as pulled pork, egg, vegetables and broth. Cocktails and good selection of Japanese beer. Excellent staff.

TRIO RESTAURANT
1537 17th St. NW, Washington, DC: 202-232-6305
www.triodc.com
CUISINE: American
DRINKS: Full bar
SERVING: Lunch, Dinner, Brunch
PRICE RANGE: $$
Neighborhood diner with outdoor seating. Typical diner food but specials shine. Good friendly service. A favorite of locals so you know it's good. Best bets are the Trio sliders, wild mushroom ravioli, and fish Spanish style. Burgers are also a good choice.

THE UGLY MUG
723 8th Street, SE, Washington, DC, 202-547-8459
www.uglymugdc.com
CUISINE: American
DRINKS: Full Bar
SERVING: Lunch, Dinner, Late Night
PRICE RANGE: $$
NEIGHBORHOOD: Capitol Hill/Barracks Row
Sports bar with great menu, has the feel of a college
bar. Menu favorites: Sliders and Buffalo Chicken.
Friendly staff.

UNION MARKET
1309 5th St NE, Washington, DC, 301-347-3998
www.unionmarketdc.com
Union Market is an artisanal food market with over
40 local vendors from up and coming to established
restaurateurs. Some of the venues include:
Rappahannock Oyster Co., Buffalo & Bergen,
Righteous Cheese, Peregrine Espresso, Lyon Bakery,

Trickling Springs Creamery, Harvey's Market, Oh! Pickles, Almaala Farms, DC Empanadas and TaKorean. Wonderful place to spend half a day. (Or even a full day.)

URBANA
2121 P St. N.W. Hotel Palomar, Washington, DC: 202-956-6650
www.urbanadc.com
CUISINE: Italian
DRINKS: Full bar
SERVING: Lunch, Dinner
PRICE RANGE: $$
This hip Dupont Circle Italian restaurant is a neighborhood favorite. Great pizzas, delicious selection of fish dishes. Excellent choice for brunch with unlimited Belini bar. Nice variety of wines.

ZAYTINYA
701 9th St. NW, Washington, DC: 202-638-0800
www.zaytinya.com
CUISINE: Turkish, Greek,
DRINKS: Full bar
SERVING: Lunch, Dinner
PRICE RANGE: $$$
Great place to take out-of-town guests. Beautiful
interior with two-level dining area. Menu favorites
include: Labneh, Tzatziki, Htipiti, Tabouleh,
Kolokithokeftedes (zucchini fritters), Seared
Halloumi Cheese, Mushroom Couscous, Patates
Tiganites Me Yiaourti (French fries) and Havuç
Köftesi (carrot apricot fritters). Great vegetarian
selections.

Chapter 5
WHERE TO SHOP

DID YOU FIND AN INTERESTING PLACE?
If you discover a place you think I should check out
on my next visit, drop me a line, will you? I'll
mention your name if I end up listing it.
andrewdelaplaine@mac.com

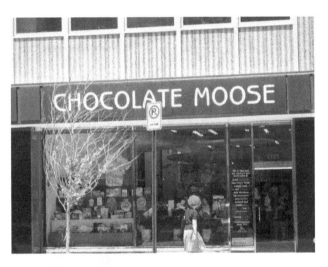

CHOCOLATE MOOSE
1743 L St. NW, Washington, DC: 202-463-0992
www.chocolatemoosedc.com
This funky gift shop has everything from beautiful to
tacky including artful accessories, bizarre books,
campy cards, cool clothing, hip housewares, jazzy
jewelry, toys, and yes, chocolate.

COLUMBIA PIKE FARMERS MARKET
2800 Columbia Pike, Arlington, VA, 703-892-2776
https://www.columbia-pike.org/
Sundays: 9am-1pm Year Round
A popular Sunday shopping spot. Here you'll find farm fresh products, free-range pork and fresh baked items like zucchini bread.

THE DAILY RIDER
600 H St NE, Washington, DC, 202-396-0704
www.thedailyriderdc.com
NEIGHBORHOOD: H Street
A one-stop shop for the urban cyclist selling bikes and stylish accessories.

DGS DELICATESSEN
1317 Connecticut Ave. NW, Washington DC, 202-293-4400
www.dgsdelicatessen.com
NEIGHBORHOOD: Dupont Circle

A tribute to the mom-and-pop grocery stores of yesterday, this grocery/deli carries everything from 8-day house cured pastrami to duck fat matzo balls. Everything served in the spirit of the old world Jewish kitchen.

KRAMERBOOKS & AFTERWORDS CAFÉ
1517 Connecticut Ave. NW, Washington, DC: 202-387-1400
www.kramers.com
Book lovers take note. Kramerbooks is not only one of the city's most beloved independent booksellers but was the first Bookstore/Cafe in the country to feature cappuccino, espresso, a full bar and food. Buy a book, eat, drink and hangout.

Washington Blade | Michael Key

MITCHELL GOLD + BOB WILLIAMS
1526 14th St. NW, Washington, DC: 202-332-3433
www.mgbwhome.com
This chain furniture shore, founded by a same-sex couple, offers retro styling with a modern twist. Great designs, upholstery, tables & storage, lighting, rugs, accessories and photography at better prices than competitors like Design Within Reach.

TABLETOP
1608 20th St. NW, Washington, DC: 202-387-7117
www.tabletopdc.com
Great place to find that unique gift but beware you won't be able to leave without buying something for yourself. Here you'll find that weird or unusual item that you didn't know you desperately needed. Cards, accessories, jewelry, and home décor.

UNION MARKET

1309 5th St NE, Washington, DC, 301-347-3998
www.unionmarketdc.com
NEIGHBORHOOD: Brentwood Park
Union Market is an artisanal food market with over
40 local vendors from up and coming to established
restaurateurs. Some of the venues include:
Rappahannock Oysters Co., Buffalo & Bergen,
Righteous Cheese, Peregrine Espresso, Lyon Bakery,
Trickling Springs Creamery, Harvey's Market, Oh!
Pickles, Almaala Farms, DC Empanadas and
TaKorean.

Chapter 6
NIGHTLIFE

DID YOU FIND AN INTERESTING PLACE?
If you discover a place you think I should check out
on my next visit, drop me a line, will you? I'll
mention your name if I end up listing it.
andrewdelaplaine@mac.com

U Street is a happening place for nightlife in
Washington. Adams Morgan used to be the busiest,
but now there's lot of activity on U.

THE BRIXTON
901 U St NW, Washington, DC, 202-560-5045
www.brixtondc.com
NEIGHBORHOOD: U Street
Trendy multi-level hangout – first floor British pub,
second floor lounge and roof deck with two bars. It
all feels very much like a British country hunting
lodge with deer antler chandeliers, old black-and-
white pictures from the past. This place attracts a
crowd of regulars. Bar menu of snacks like sliders,
calamari and burgers.

CHURCHKEY
1337 14th St NW, Washington, DC, 202-567-2576.
www.churchkeydc.com
NEIGHBORHOOD: Logan Circle
Located near the galleries on 14th Street, this place
has an unbelievable beer selection with 50 on draft

and over 500 in bottles. Bar menu with items like mac n cheese and the brat burger.

H STREET COUNTRY CLUB
1335 H St NE, Washington, DC, 202-399-4722
www.thehstreetcountryclub.com
NEIGHBORHOOD: H Street Corridor
Essentially this is a bar with lots of games including miniature golf. Multiple bars, rooftop patio. Drink specials.

THE GIBSON
2009 14th St. NW, Washington: 202-232-2156
thegibsondc.com/

They offer experienced mixologists here, so come for the swanky cocktail creations. Perfect place for a romantic get together: dark, lots of candles, appropriate music. Only holds 50 people at the bar and at a few tables. Because it's popular and they do not allow you to stand around the way they do in other bars, you have to reserve to get in on busy nights. If you show up without a reservation, you give your cell # to the doorman who will call you when space opens up. Unusual, huh? While you wait, you can drift off to nearby watering holes to explore. (Not usually a wait Sunday-Thursday.)

MARTIN'S TAVERN
1264 Wisconsin Ave. NW, Washington, DC, 202-333-7370;
www.martinstavern.com
NEIGHBORHOOD: Georgetown

A historic family-owned tavern with mismatched Tiffany-style lamps hanging over the mahogany bar. American menu serves items like Richard M. Nixon's favorite meatloaf and President Truman's preferred pot roast.

OFF THE RECORD AT THE HAY-ADAMS
800 16th St NW, Washington, DC, 202-638-6600
www.hayadams.com
NEIGHBORHOOD: Downtown

Elegant old bar with wooden furniture and ornate walls covered with pictures, drawings and charicatures of politicians, current and past, with colorful interpretations of the subjects. Bar serves classic coctails (like Manhattans and Old Fashioneds) any pol would love. Nice bar menu.

ROUND ROBIN BAR
WILLARD HOTEL
1401 Pennsylvania Ave NW, Washington, 202-637-7348
https://washington.intercontinental.com
NEIGHBORHOOD: Penn Quarter
Located in the luxury Willard Hotel, this upscale, century-old lounge serves classic cocktails. Old school ambiance. Nice menu of bar nibbles. Legend has it that Ulysses S. Grant coining the term "lobbyists" as a label for those who chased after him

in the Willard's lobby beseeching him for jobs in his Administration. (Ask the bartender about the artist who drew the illustrations on the walls—very interesting story.)

ST REGIS BAR
The St. Regis
923 16th St NW, Washington, 202-638-2626
www.stregiswashingtondc.com
NEIGHBORHOOD: Downtown
Located inside the St. Regis Hotel, this beautifully decorated lounge serves up handcrafted cocktails and a menu of upscale bar snacks. This classic bar is an ideal stop for cocktails, light bites and conversation, not to mention people watching if you're into high rollers and DC power types.

THE TOMBS
1226 36th St. NW, Washington, DC, 202-337-6668
www.tombs.com

NEIGHBORHOOD: Georgetown
Since 1962, The Tombs has been a popular gathering place for Georgetown students. TVs for watching the game. Also popular spot for Sunday brunch.

U STREET MUSIC HALL
1115 U St. NW (bet. 11th & 12th), Washington: 202-588-1889
www.ustreetmusichall.com
DJs actually own and operate this dance club that holds about 500 people (more if the Fire Marshall's not looking). 1200-sq.-ft. cork cushioned dance floor. Here you'll find DJs keeping the pace frenzied till the late hours. Everybody agrees this is the best dance club in the whole area. Best light & sound system, best vibe, best everything, and not pretentious.

Chapter 7
WHAT TO SEE & DO

DID YOU FIND AN INTERESTING PLACE?
If you discover a place you think I should check out on my next visit, drop me a line, will you? I'll mention your name if I end up listing it.
andrewdelaplaine@mac.com

ADAMSON GALLERY
926 N St NW Suite #2, Washington, DC, 202-232-0707
www.adamsongallery.com

Founded in 1982, this is one of Washington DC's leading contemporary galleries exhibiting the talents of outstanding international artists. This gallery has an impressive roster of artists including Chuck Close, Annie Leibovitz, Robert Longo, Jim Hodges, and William Wegman.

ARLINGTON HOUSE - ROBERT E. LEE MEMORIAL
321 Sherman Dr, Ft Myer, VA, 703-235-1530
www.nps.gov/arho
Once the home of Confederate General Robert E. Lee, this Greek revival style Mansion overlooks the Potomac River and the National Mall. This former 1,100-acre estate featured a gorgeous mansion and fields maintained by slaves. The mansion built by George Washington Parke Curtis, Martha Washington's grandson between 1802 and 1818. Visitors can tour the Arlington House, The Robert E. Lee Memorial, the Robert E. Lee Museum, and the slave quarters. The mansion features exhibits about the life of Robert E. Lee. Free admission.

ARLINGTON NATIONAL CEMETERY
Arlington, VA, 877-907-8585
www.arlingtoncemetery.org
A 624-acre United States military cemetery that has more than three million visitors every year. This cemetery is the final resting place for deceased veterans of many of the nation's wars beginning with the American Civil War. Visitors should first stop at the Welcome Center, located by the cemetery

entrance, where maps, exhibits, information services, a bookstore and restrooms are located.

ATLAS PERFORMING ARTS CENTER
1333 H St. NE, Washington, DC, 202-399-7993
www.atlasarts.org
NEIGHBORHOOD: H Street Corridor/Atlas District
This multiple space performing arts facility is a popular attraction offering music, dance, theatre, film and multimedia performances. On-site café serving drinks and snacks.

BASILICA OF THE NATIONAL SHRINE OF THE IMMACULATE CONCEPTION
400 Michigan Avenue, NE, Washington, DC: 202-526-8300
www.nationalshrine.com
ADMISSION: Free
HOURS: April 1 - October 31, 7 am - 7 pm
November 1 - March 31, 7 am - 6 pm
The Basilica of the National Shrine of the Immaculate Conception is the largest Roman Catholic Church in the United

States and North America, and is one of the ten largest churches in the world. Designated by the United States Conference of Catholic Bishops as a National Sanctuary of Prayer and Pilgrimage, the Basilica is the nation's preeminent Marian shrine, dedicated to the patroness of the United States—the Blessed Virgin Mary under her title of the Immaculate Conception. Over one million people visit every year. The Basilica has been visited by Pope Benedict XVI, Pope John Paul II, and Mother Teresa, and rivals the great sanctuaries of Europe and the world. Byzantine-Romanesque in style, its massive, one-of-a-kind superstructure is home to over 70 chapels and oratories that relate to the peoples, cultures and traditions that are the fabric of the Catholic faith and the mosaic of our great nation. The Basilica also houses the largest collection of contemporary ecclesiastical art on earth.

Free parking, guided tours, a gift shop, bookstore, and cafeteria.

BATTLEGROUND NATIONAL CEMETERY
6625 Georgia Ave. NW, Washington, DC, 202-895-6000
NEIGHBORHOOD: Brightwood
This is a small cemetery hidden on Georgia Avenue where the soldiers who died in the battle of Fort Stevens. More than 900 soldiers were killed or wounded during that battle. After the Confederates retreated on July 12, Union troops buried 40 of the soldiers in a peach orchard that had been part of the battlefield. That night, Lincoln dedicated the one-acre cemetery, one of the smallest national cemeteries in the country. Visitors can see the 41 graves, the last grave belongs to Major Edward R. Campbell - the last Union survivor of the battle, the restored lodge and a marble rostrum added in 1921.

THE CAPITOL BUILDING
East Capitol St NE & First St SE, Washington, DC
202-226-8000
www.visitthecapitol.gov
HOURS: tours run from 9 to 4:30, and last 45
minutes, Monday through Saturday. The earlier you
go, the shorter the wait will be.

THE CAPITAL WHEEL
116 Waterfront St, National Harbor, MD, 301-842-
8650
www.thecapitalwheel.com
ADMISSION: Admission Fee applies

Popular Americana-themed 36-foot carousel set on the waterfront. Carousel holds 42 climate-controlled gondolas (each holds 8 people) including one VIP gondola (that only holds 4). From the top you can see the Washington Monument, U.S. Capitol, Alexandria and Prince George's County. Length of ride: 12 – 15 minutes.

CHURCH OF THE EPIPHANY
1317 G St. NW, Washington, DC, 202-347-2635
www.epiphanydc.org
Built in 1844, the Church of the Epiphany, one of the few remaining pre-Civil War churches in DC. Before the war, Confederate President Jefferson Davis was a member of this church. In 1863, the building became a temporary hospital for the wounded.

DC BY FOOT TOURS
Washington, DC, 202-370-1830
www.freetoursbyfoot.com/washington-dc-tours
A unique tour company that offers "name your own price" and some free walking tours of Washington, DC. Tours take you anywhere from the National Mall to DC neighborhoods, to the monuments, cemeteries, the Pentagon and Georgetown. The tours led by expert guides show you the interesting side of DC. Also available: private group tours, bus tours, and ghost tours. Tours are free but tipping is welcomed.

DISTRICT OF COLUMBIA COURT OF APPEALS
500 Indiana Ave. NW, #6000, Washington, DC
www.dccourts.gov/internet/appellate/main.jsf

This Greek Revival building, built between 1820 and 1850, served as Washington's City Hall until 1871. Now it houses D.C.'s Court of Appeals.

DONALD W. REYNOLDS CENTER FOR AMERICAN ART AND PORTRAITURE
Eighth and F streets NW, Washington, DC, 202-633-7970
www.americanart.si.edu/reynolds_center
More than 3,000 works of art are exhibited on two balconied levels of the beautiful Victorian embellished Great Hall courtesy of The Luce Foundation Center for American Art. Museum store. Free admission.

DUMBARTON OAKS
1703 32nd St. NW, Washington, DC, 202-339-6401
www.doaks.org
NEIGHBORHOOD: Georgetown

An 1801 red-brick museum/research laboratory that was formerly the home and gardens of Robert Woods Bliss and his wife Mildred. Visitors are allowed entrance to the historic estate & gardens and to view the world-class collections of art. The museum's Music Room offers lectures and concerts. Small admission fee.

FOLGER SHAKESPEARE LIBRARY

201 E. Capitol St. SE, Washington DC: 202-544-7077
www.folger.edu
ADMISSION: Free
HOURS: The Folger is open to the public Monday through Saturday from 10 a.m. to 5 p.m. and Sunday from Noon to 5 p.m.

The Folger Shakespeare Library, located on Capitol Hill in Washington, DC, is home to the world's largest and finest collection of Shakespeare materials and to major collections of other rare Renaissance books, manuscripts, and works of art. The Folger opened in 1932 and continues to serve a wide audience of researchers, visitors, teachers, students, families, and theater- and concert-goers. The Folger is a world-renowned research center on Shakespeare with a conservation lab that is a leading innovator in the preservation of rare materials. The Folger offers public programs that include plays, concerts, literary readings, family activities, and exhibitions.

FORD'S THEATRE

511 Tenth St. NW, Washington, DC: 202-347-4833
www.fordstheatre.org
ADMISSION: Free
HOURS: 9 am to 5 pm

Ford's Theatre is a National Historic Site and museum devoted to Lincoln's presidency, and an active theater putting on a full season of shows every year. The museum, redesigned and reopened July 15, 2009, uses historic artifacts, environmental recreations, videos, and sculptural figures to tell the story of the election of 1860, Lincoln's cabinet, the conduct of the war, the Gettysburg Address, the election of 1864 and the second inauguration, and the assassination. It was here that Lincoln was assassinated on April 14, 1865.

FORT STEVENS

13th and Quackenbos streets NW, Washington, DC, 202-895-6000

www.nps.gov/cwdw/historyculture/fort-stevens.htm

This partially reconstructed Fort is a favorite stop for Civil War enthusiasts. Originally called Fort Massachusetts, the For was later named Fort Stevens after Brig. General Isaac Ingalls Stevens who was killed at the Battle of Chantilly.

FORT WARD MUSEUM AND HISTORIC SITE

4301 W. Braddock Rd., Alexandria, VA, 703-838-4848

www.alexandriava.gov/FortWard

Although it never experienced enemy fire during the Civil War, Fort Ward was the fifth largest fort built to defend Washington, DC. Today it has been well-preserved with nearly 95% of its earthen walls intact. The site is also the setting of Civil War reenactments several times a year. There is also a museum that covers daily life and Civil War medical care. The Museum and Historic Fort are located within a 45-acre park. Free admission.

THE FRANKLIN DELANO ROOSEVELT MEMORIAL

1850 West Basin Dr SW, Washington, DC, 202-426-6841

www.nps.gov/fdrm

A memorial dedicated to the memory of President Frankly Delano Roosevelt.

The memorial, located on the CherryTree Walk, covers about 7 ½ acres. The memorial consists of four outdoor rooms, one for
each of FDR's terms. The memorial also includes a timeline of

dates during Roosevelt's life. An information center and bookstore are located at the entrance of the memorial. Free admission.

HEMPHILL FINE ARTS
434 K St NW, Washington, DC, 202-234-5601
www.hemphillfinearts.com
NEIGHBORHOOD: Logan Circle
Since 1993, Hemphell Fine Arts has been exhibiting contemporary art from emerging to mid-career and established artists. This gallery is known for mounting socially relevant exhibitions appealing to a broad range of interests.

HILLWOOD MUSEUM & GARDENS
4155 Linnean Ave. NW, Washington, DC: 202-686-5807
www.hillwoodmuseum.org
ADMISSION: $15 suggested donation
HOURS: Tuesday to Saturday 10 am to 5 pm
Hillwood is an urban oasis that blends exquisite arts and lush gardens. The former residence of businesswoman, diplomat, philanthropist and collector Marjorie Merriweather Post, the collection focuses heavily on the House of Romanov. Included are Fabergé eggs and 18th and 19th century French art and one of the country's finest orchid collections.

HILLYER ART SPACE
9 Hillyer Court NW, Washington, DC, 202-338-0680
www.artsandartists.org
NEIGHBORHOOD: Dupont Circle
Great art space that hosts a Friday open house with wine and music. Popular gallery space and event site. Attracts a young trendy crowd.

THE HOWARD THEATRE
620 T St. NW, Washington DC: 202-803-2899
www.thehowardtheatre.com
ADMISSION: Tickets for performances can be purchased through the box office.
The Howard Theatre is a historic theatre, located at 620 T Street, Northwest, Washington, D.C. Opened in 1910, it was added to the National Register of Historic Places in 1974. Once known for catering to an African-American clientele and hosting many of

the great black musical artists of the early and mid-twentieth century, today the theatre offers headline acts like Wanda Sykes, Blue Oyster Cult, and Chaka Khan.

JEFFERSON MEMORIAL
701 E Basin Dr SW, Washington, DC: 202-426-6841
www.nps.gov/thje
ADMISSION: Free
HOURS: Open to the public 24 hours a day. Rangers are on duty to answer questions from 9:30 a.m. to 11:30 pm daily and to provide interpretive programs every hour on the hour from 10 a.m. until 11 pm
Presidential memorial dedicated to Thomas Jefferson, an American Founding Father and the third President of the United States. The neoclassical building was designed by the architect John Russell Pope and built by the Philadelphia contractor John

McShain. Construction of the building began in 1938 and was completed in 1943. The bronze statue of Jefferson was added in 1947. Ranked fourth on the List of America's Favorite Architecture by the American Institute of Architects.

JOHN F. KENNEDY CENTER FOR THE PERFORMING ARTS

2700 F St. NW, Washington, DC: 800-444-1324
www.kennedy-center.org
ADMISSION: Free guided tour, 10 am to 5 pm
HOURS: Mon-Sun, 10 am–9 pm
The John F. Kennedy Center for the Performing Arts, commonly referred to as the Kennedy Center, is a performing arts center located on the Potomac River, adjacent to the Watergate complex. The Center, also known as America's National Cultural Center, houses and produces theater, dance, ballet, orchestral, chamber, jazz, popular, and folk music. Designed by architect Edward Durell Stone, it was built by Philadelphia contractor John McShain and is administered by a bureau of the Smithsonian Institution. The Center has three main theatres: a Concert Hall, an Opera House and the Eisenhower Theater. Other venues include the Terrace Theater, the Theater Lab, and the Millennium Stage. There are two restaurants on site. Free daily performances are held on the Millennium Stage in the Grand Foyer.

KING - DR. MARTIN LUTHER KING, JR. NATIONAL MEMORIAL
1964 Independence Ave., SW, Washington, DC, 202-426-6841
www.nps.gov/mlkm
ADMISSION: Free
HOURS: Open 24 hours
Located at the northwest corner of the Tidal Basin near the Franklin Delano Roosevelt Memorial, on a sightline linking the Lincoln Memorial to the northwest and the Jefferson Memorial to the southeast. Covering four acres, the memorial opened on August 22, 2011. Dr. King is the first African-American honored with a memorial on or near the National Mall and only the fourth non-President with such a memorial. Lei Yixin was the designer of the sculpture.

THE KOREAN WAR VETERANS MEMORIAL
900 Ohio Dr. SW, Washington, 202-426-6841

www.nps.gov/kwvm
This inspiring memorial, located in West Potomac Park along the National Mall, southeast of the Lincoln Memorial, pays tribute those who served in the Korean War. Park staff offers daily interpretive tours every hour from 10 a.m – 11 p.m. Free admission.

THE KREEGER MUSEUM

2401 Foxhall Rd NW, Washington DC: 202-337-3050 ext. 10
www.kreegermuseum.org
ADMISSION: Adults $10, Members of the military (with ID) $7, Students (with ID) $7, Seniors (65+) $7, Children (12 & under) and Members Free.
HOURS: Tuesday-Thursday - Reservations required for admittance. Guests must sign up for the 10:30 am or 1:30 p.m. guided tour. Call 202-338-3552 or email visitorservices@kreegermuseum.org. Friday & Saturday: Open 10 a.m. to 4 p.m. No reservations needed. Optional guided tours at 10:30 & 1:30 on Fridays; 10:30, 12:00 & 2:00 on Saturdays. Closed Sundays, Mondays and the month of August.
The Kreeger Museum is a private, non-profit art museum located in the former residence of David and Carmen Kreeger, set within five and a half acres of sculpture-filled gardens and tranquil woods. Designed by renowned architect Philip Johnson, this is one of the few examples of his work in DC. The Museum's focus on 19th and 20th century paintings can be seen through works by Monet, Picasso, Renoir, Cézanne, Chagall, Miró, and Stella, along with prominent Washington artists. Also included in the collection are

outstanding examples of traditional African and Asian art.

THE LIBRARY OF CONGRESS

101 Independence Ave. SE, Washington DC: 202-707-5000

www.loc.gov

ADMISSION: Free

HOURS: All buildings are closed to the public on Sundays, Thanksgiving Day, Christmas and New Year's Holidays. The Madison and Adams buildings are closed on all federal holidays. In the event of inclement weather or other issues, the Library of Congress follows the Federal Government operating status.

Thomas Jefferson Building: Great Hall and Exhibitions – Mon. – Sat. 8:30 a.m. - 4:30 p.m. CLOSED Thanksgiving Day, Christmas and New Years Holidays.

The Library of Congress is the world's largest collection of knowledge, culture, and creativity. Located in four buildings in Washington, D.C., as well as the Packard Campus in Culpeper, Virginia, this is the largest library in the world by shelf space and number of books. The Library of Congress was housed in the U.S. Capitol for most of the 19th century. Library of Congress has more than 32 million cataloged books and other print materials in 470 languages; more than 61 million manuscripts; the largest rare book collection in North America, including the rough draft of the Declaration of Independence, and a Gutenberg Bible (one of only four perfect vellum copies known to exist). The

Library also holds over 1 million U.S. government publications; 1 million issues of world newspapers spanning the past three centuries; 33,000 bound newspaper volumes; 500,000 microfilm reels; over 6,000 comic book titles; films; 5.3 million maps; 6 million works of sheet music; 3 million sound recordings; more than 14.7 million prints and photographic images including fine and popular art pieces and architectural drawings; the Betts Stradivarius; and the Cassavetti Stradivarius.

LINCOLN COTTAGE AT THE SOLDIERS' HOME

140 Rock Creek Church Rd NW, Washington, DC, 202-829-0436
www.lincolncottage.org
President Lincoln's Cottage, located on the grounds of the Soldiers' home, is a national monument. The cottage was originally built in 1842. Guests can take a tour with explores Lincoln's road to emancipation which culminated at the cottage. Small admission ticket includes guided tour.

LINCOLN MEMORIAL AND REFLECTING POOL

2 Lincoln Memorial Cir NW, Washington, 202-426-6841
ADMISSION: Free
HOURS: Open 24 hours.
Lincoln Memorial Reflecting Pool is the largest of many reflecting pools in DC.
Located on the National Mall, directly east of the Lincoln Memorial, with the Washington Monument

to the east of the reflecting pool. Part of the iconic image of Washington, the reflecting pool hosts many of the 24 million visitors a year who visit the National Mall. The pool dramatically reflects the Washington Monument, the Lincoln Memorial, the Mall's trees, and/or the expansive sky. The Lincoln Memorial is an American national monument built to honor the 16th President of the United States, Abraham Lincoln. The architect was Henry Bacon, the sculptor of the primary statue – Abraham Lincoln, 1920 – was Daniel Chester French, and the painter of the interior murals was Jules Guerin. The building, in the form of a Greek Doric temple, contains a large seated sculpture of Abraham Lincoln and inscriptions of two well-known speeches by Lincoln, The Gettysburg Address and his Second Inaugural Address. The site of many famous speeches, including Martin Luther King's "I Have a Dream" speech, delivered on August 28, 1963 during the rally at the end of the March on Washington for Jobs and Freedom.

THE MALL
The whole point of a visit to Washington is to see some of the places lining the Mall, that grassy area which runs from the U.S. Capitol Building down to the Washington Monument.

MERIDIAN HILL PARK
2400 15th St NW, Washington, DC, 202-895-6000
www.nps.gov/mehi
NEIGHBORHOOD: Columbus Heights
This popular park, unofficially known as "Malcolm X Park", is located directly north of the White House.

Designed in the 1930s, the main feature of this park is the Neoclassical waterfall.

NATIONAL AIR AND SPACE MUSEUM
600 Independence Ave SW, Washington, DC, 202-633-2214
www.airandspace.si.edu
A favorite stop for the kids. This is the largest of the Smithsonian's 19 museums and one of the most kid-friendly branches of the Smithsonian with a variety of exhibits and shows including a 20-minute planetarium show starring Sesame Street characters. Here you'll see vintage flying machines like Charles Lindburgh's 1927 Spirit of St. Louis and the 1969 Apollo 11 command module. The collection features some 60,000 objects including Saturn V rockets, jetliners, gliders, and space helmets. One-third of the Museum's aircraft and spacecraft are one-of-a-kind. Great museum store for gifts and souvenirs. Free admission.

NATIONAL BUILDING MUSEUM

401 F St. NW, Washington, DC, 202-272-2448
www.nbm.org

Historically known as the Pension Building, the National Building Museum celebrates architecture, design, engineering, construction, and urban planning. Located next to the National Law Enforcement Officers Memorial and the Judiciary Square Metro station. The museum hosts a variety of temporary exhibitions in galleries around the Great Hall. The museum also hosts public programs, family festivals, and tours. The museum's lecture series features architects and designers from around the world. Built in the 1880s, this post-Civil War structure is a landmark because of the war and while it housed the U.S. Pensions Bureau millions of dollars were dispersed to veterans.

NATIONAL GALLERY OF ART

6th Constitution Ave NW, Washington, DC: 202-737-4215

www.nga.gov
ADMISSION: Free
HOURS: Open Monday through Saturday from 10 am to 5 pm and Sunday from 11 am to 6 pm. The Gallery is closed on December 25 and January 1. Located on the National Mall, the National Gallery of Art is one of the world's greatest art museums. Comprised of two buildings - one exhibits paintings from the 13th through the 18th centuries and the other exhibits modern art. The Gallery's collection of paintings, drawings, prints, photographs, sculpture, medals, and decorative arts traces the development of Western Art from the Middle Ages to the present, including the only painting by Leonardo da Vinci in the Americas and the largest mobile ever created by Alexander Calder. The Gallery includes the original neoclassical West Building designed by John Russell Pope that is linked underground to the modern East Building, designed by I. M. Pei. Galleries in the West Building that exhibit Impressionism and Post-Impressionism have reopened after 2 years of renovations. Here you'll see one of the greatest collections of paintings by Manet, Monet, Renoir, Cezanne, Van Gogh and Gauguin. The gallery's latest 19th Century will return to public view in as freshly conceived installation design. Sculpture garden, gift shop.

NATIONAL MUSEUM OF NATURAL HISTORY - SMITHSONIAN INSTITUTION
10th St. & Constitution Ave. NW, Washington, DC
202-633-1000
www.mnh.si.edu

HOURS: Daily 10 a.m.-5:30 p.m. Summer hours are extended to 7:30 p.m. from Memorial Day to Labor Day, unless the museum has a special event scheduled. Check the museum's Web site for details. METRO: Smithsonian Station (Orange, Blue lines); also the Circulator bus.

Emphasis here is on biology, geology and anthropology. The collections are quite vast, but the old-style dioramas will remind you of your first school visit to a museum when you were a kid. Still, they have their charm.

On the first floor, after you pass a huge African elephant on entering, you can see 270+ species of stuffed mammals, fossils and dinosaurs.

No visit is complete without a swing into **The Discovery Room,** a lots-of-fun interactive room for kids and families.

The second floor houses exhibitions featuring minerals and gems, including the Hope Diamond.

Also on site are an IMAX theatre, restaurant and shop.

Opened in 1910.

NATIONAL MUSEUM OF THE AMERICAN INDIAN

4th St & Independence Ave SW, Washington, DC, 202-633-1000

www.nmai.si.edu

This museum houses one of the world's largest and diverse collections pertaining to the American Indian. Impressive exhibitions presented in collaboration with American Indian tribes and communities. Free admission. Stop at the museum's Mitsitam Native Foods Cafe and experience some delicious Native foods found throughout the Western Hemisphere like fly bread and corn totopos. Museum store is also worth a visit with an nice variety of jewelry, textiles, Native American souvenirs, books and toys.

NATIONAL WORLD WAR II MEMORIAL

17th St SW, Washington, DC, 202-208-3818

www.wwiimemorial.com

The World War II Memorial is a monument honoring the 16 million who served in the armed forces during World War II. This memorial is open to visitors 24 hours a day, seven days a week.

NATIONAL ZOOLOGICAL PARK
3001 Connecticut Ave NW, Washington, D.C., 202-633-4888
www.nationalzoo.si.edu
The National Zoological Park, known as the National Zoo, is one of the oldest zoos in the United States. This 163 acre park houses more than 2,000 animals of 400 different species including giant pandas, bears, lions, giraffes, tigers, monkeys, sea lions, and more. Wear comfortable shoes as this is a walking experience. Free admission but there is a fee for parking.

NATIONALS PARK
1500 South Capitol St SE, Washington, DC, 202-675-6287
http://washington.nationals.mlb.com/was/ballpark/index.jsp
Nationals Park, hoe to the Washington Nationals, is a well-known baseball park located along the Anacostia River in the Navy Yard neighborhood. Site of other big-arena sporting events as well.

OLD TOWN TROLLEY TOURS
50 Massachusetts Ave NE, Washington, DC, 202-832-9800
www.trolleytours.com

Old Town Trolley Tours offers one of the best ways to see DC with 20 stops and highlighting more than 100 points of interest. Friendly conductors take you share the country's rich history and even present day facts about DC. Admission fee allows you to jump on and jump off the trolley tour all day. Fee includes tour map with all stops listed and things to do at each stop. Shuttles to major attractions.

PASSPORT DC
Cultural Tourism DC
1250 H Street, NW, Washington, DC, 202-661-7581
www.culturaltourismdc.org
Every year during May, Cultural Tourism DC presents a month-long celebration of international culture called Passport DC. This series of events showcases Washington DC's embassies and cultural organizations with a variety of performances, talks, open houses, tours, and exhibitions. Several DC museums participate in Passport DC programming. This series offers an inside look at many international embassies that are generally off-limits. Check website for schedule. Free events.

THE PHILLIPS COLLECTION
1600 21st St. NW, Washington, DC: 202-387-2151
www.phillipscollection.org
ADMISSION: Adults $12, Students $10, seniors 62
and over $10.
HOURS: Tues-Sat, 10 am –5 pm; Sunday, 11 am–6
pm; Thurs. extended hours 5 – 8:30 pm. Closed
Mondays, New Year's Day, Independence Day,
Thanksgiving Day, Christmas Eve, and Christmas
Day
The Phillips Collection building comprises the
original Phillips house built in 1897 and two major
additions: the Goh Annex, built in 1960 and enlarged
in 1989, and the Sant Building, opened in 2006. The
artists represented in the collection are Pierre-Auguste
Renoir, Gustave Courbet, El Greco, Vincent van
Gogh, Henri Matisse, Claude Monet, Pablo Picasso,
Georges Braque, Pierre Bonnard, Paul Klee, Arthur
Dove, Winslow Homer, James McNeill Whistler,
Jacob Lawrence, Augustus Vincent Tack, Georgia
O'Keeffe, and Mark Rothko. Museum gift shop offers
hundreds of art related items.

POTOMAC RIVERBOAT COMPANY
205 The Strand, Alexandria, VA, 703-684-0580
www.potomacriverboatco.com
A private cruise company, owned by the Polak family for over 30 years, that offers quick cruises down the river, narrated tours, and water taxis.

SMITHSONIAN CAROUSEL
900 Jefferson Dr. SW, Washington, DC, 202-633-1000
www.nationalcarousel.com
Located in front of the Arts and Industries Building on the National Mall. Old fashioned carousel built in the 1940s. Open daily. Small admission fee for three-minute ride.

SMITHSONIAN INSTITUTION
3001 Connecticut Avenue NW, 202-633-1000
www.si.edu

ADMISSION: Free

The Smithsonian Institution is the world's largest museum complex and research organization with 19 museums and the National Zoo. It's difficult to choose which ones you'll take in on a short trip, so focus on what interests you most. Venues include: African American History and Culture Museum, African Art Museum, Air and Space Museum, Air and Space Museum Udvar-Hazy Center, American Art Museum, American History Museum, American Indian Museum, American Indian Museum Heye Center, Anacostia Community Museum, Arts and Industries Building, Cooper-Hewitt, National Design Museum, Freer Gallery of Art, Hirshhorn Museum and Sculpture Garden, National Zoo, Natural History Museum, Portrait Gallery, Postal Museum, Renwick Gallery, Sackler Gallery, Smithsonian Institution Building, and The Castle.

THE TEXTILE MUSEUM

701 21st Street, NW, Washington, DC: 202-994-5200

www.museum.gwu.edu/textile-museum

ADMISSION: $8 suggested donation for non-members

HOURS: Monday, Wednesday through Friday and Sunday 1 to 5 p.m. Closed Tuesdays and university holidays.

The Textile Museum celebrates public knowledge and appreciation of the artistic merits and cultural importance of the world's textiles. The Textile Museum reopened in March 2015 as part of the George Washington University Museum and The

Textile Museum on GW's main campus in Foggy Bottom.

THE TRANSFORMER GALLERY
1404 P St. NW, Washington, DC, 202-483-1102
www.transformerdc.org
This non-profit, artist-centered gallery promotes and exhibits emerging artists. Besides exhibitions the gallery also offers a series of programs and workshops.
NEIGHBORHOOD: Dupont Circle

THE U.S. NATIONAL ARCHIVES
700 Pennsylvania Ave. NW, Washington, DC: 866-272-6272
www.archives.gov
ADMISSION: Free
HOURS: Mon-Tue, Sat, 9 am–5 pm; Wed-Fri, 9 am–9 pm; Closed on Sunday.
This is where you can actually view official documents such as the Declaration of Independence, The Constitution, and Bill of Rights. You can research your family history or view World War II photos. This is an independent agency of the U.S. government that preserves and documents government and historical records. A component of the National Archives experience is the 290-seat William G. McGowan Theater that shows a short signature film about the National Archives and twice-daily shows a film about the Charters of Freedom. Archives gift shop sells copies of documents, books, and gifts.

UNITED STATES BOTANIC GARDEN

100 Maryland Ave. SW, Washington DC, DC: 202-226-8333

www.usbg.gov

ADMISSION: Free

HOURS: Mon-Sun, 10 am–5 pm

This is the oldest continually operating botanic garden in the United States. As a living plant museum it informs visitors about the importance of plants to the well being of humans and to the earths ecosystems. Open every day of the year. One of the highlights of the Garden is the historic Lord & Burnham greenhouse, built by the Architect of the Capitol in 1933, contains eight garden rooms under glass. The Botanic Garden is home to almost 10,000 living specimens, some of them over 165 years old.

VIETNAM VETERANS MEMORIAL

5 Henry Bacon Dr NW, Washington, DC, 202-426-6841

www.nps.gov/vive

This memorial, open 24 hours a day, features the names of over 58,000 servicemen and women who died during the Vietnam Conflict. This memorial also includes "The Three Servicemen" statue and the Vietnam Women's Memorial. Free admission.

WASHINGTON MONUMENT
No 2 - 15th St NW, Washington, DC: 202-426-6841
www.nps.gov/wamo
ADMISSION: Free, ticket required.
HOURS: Mon-Sun, 9 am–5 pm
Probably one of the most well known monuments in
DC, the Washington Monument is an obelisk on the
National Mall built to commemorate the first
American president, General George Washington.
The monument stands 555 feet tall and was opened to
the public in 1885.

WASHINGTON NATIONAL CATHEDRAL
3101 Wisconsin Ave. NW, Washington, DC: 202-537-6200
www.nationalcathedral.org
ADMISSION: Free. Tours available. Rates vary for
special events.
HOURS: Mon-Fri,10 am–5:30 pm; Sat, 10 am–4:30
pm; Sun, 7:30 am–4 pm
Thing to do here is get a tour of their unique carved
gargoyles. There's a great one with a man riding a
large hog while hanging onto a duck with his other
hand. Others include monsters, dogs, horses and even
Darth Vader.

The Cathedral Church of Saint Peter and Saint Paul, popularly known as Washington National Cathedral, is a cathedral of the Episcopal Church. Of neogothic design, it is the sixth-largest cathedral in the world, the second-largest in the United States, and the fourth-tallest structure in Washington, D.C. This is one of DC's popular attractions attracting nearly a half a million visitors a year. Funeral services for Dwight Eisenhower (1969), Ronald Reagan (2004) and Gerald Ford (2007) have been held in this cathedral. Reverend Martin Luther King, Jr. delivered the final Sunday sermon of his life here, just a few days before his assassination. The property includes two gardens, four schools, a greenhouse and two gift shops.

THE WHITE HOUSE
1600 Pennsylvania Ave. NW, Washington, DC: 202-456-1111
www.whitehouse.gov
In simpler times, you just had to line up and go on the tour on a first-come, first-serve basis. Not so now after 9/11. You have to request a ticket and you have to go through your congressman's office to do it. Your representative will send your name to the White house to be cleared. It's a hot ticket, so be sure to apply MONTHS in advance. You'll get an email telling you the date and time of your tour.

Once you go through security, you go on the self-guided tour of the 8 rooms open to the pubic. The rooms you get to see are small and you don't get much. Ropes bar you from actually entering the rooms. Peering through the doorway to the library, you want to be able to go up to the shelves, the way you can in Frick house in New York, but not here. The china room, set up by Mrs. Woodrow Wilson, is similarly frustrating. You can't get a good look at anything.

In the Vermeil Room, where they keep the loads of silver they've collected over the years, you again only get a peek.

If you were a foreign visitor, you'd be heartily disappointed after "touring" the chief executive's residence/office. I was.

When you go to the second floor, you get to see the East Room, used for large receptions, and the State Dining room, where the President might host a sit-down dinner for visiting heads of state. The more modest reception rooms, known by their colors— Blue, red and Green—look a lot like your rich grandmother's living room. Musty and not used much. The good thing is you get to enter these rooms, but ropes keep you away from the glass and furniture.

One thing they don't put in the brochure: the views from the windows of these rooms. Take a look out one and you'll see the Jefferson Memorial. You'll remember what you see through the windows much more than what you see in the rooms.

Secret Service agents stationed in each room will give you historical anecdotes if you ask them. They're trained for this.

There's a **Visitor Center,** across from the southeast gate, near the Commerce Building. Here, you can see a documentary that runs continuously showing how the house has changed visually over the years.

The White House is one of the world's most famous buildings and the official residence and principal workplace of the President of the United States. Designed by James Hoban and built between 1792 and 1800 in white-painted Aquia Creed sandstone in the Neoclassical style. Every president since John Adams has lived here. Public tours of the White House are available but requests must be submitted through one's Member of Congress.

THE WINDER BUILDING
600 17th St NW, Washington, 202-395-3000
When it opened in 1848, this five-story building towered over most of its neighbors and was touted as "Washington's first skyscraper." During the Civil War, Generals Winfield Scott and Ulysses S. Grant had offices here. Today the building is not open to the public.

YARDS PARK
355 Water St. SE, Washington DC: 202-465-7080
www.yardspark.org
ADMISSION: Free
HOURS: Open daily from 7 a.m. until two hours after sunset. Typically 7-8 p.m. (winter) or 10 p.m. (summer).

DC's new waterfront destination and centerpiece of the Capitol Riverfront neighborhood. Located just south of Capitol Hill and to the east of Nationals Ballpark, this thoughtfully designed park is a place to be active or relax and enjoy open grassy areas and well-landscaped outdoor rooms, a waterfall and a canal-like water feature, an elevated overlook, an iconic bridge and light sculpture, terraced performance venue, and a riverfront boardwalk.

INDEX

Meltzer, Daniel Silva, Don DeLillo
If you like these TV series –
House of Cards, Scandal, West Wing, The Good
Wife, Madam Secretary, Designated Survivor

You'll love the **unputdownable** series about
Jack Houston St. Clair, with political intrigue, romance,
and loads of action and suspense.

Besides writing travel books, I've written political
thrillers for many years that have delighted hundreds
of thousands of readers. I want to introduce you to my
work!
Send me an email and I'll send you a link where you
can download the first 3 books in my bestselling
series, absolutely FREE.
Mention **this book** when you email me.

andrewdelaplaine@mac.com

CPSIA information can be obtained
at www.ICGtesting.com
Printed in the USA
BVHW040836221221
624590BV00016BA/629